THE BACKPACKER'S COOKBOOK

A PRACTICAL GUIDE TO DINING OUT

D0318633

DAVE COUSTICK

www.theinpinn.co.uk

an imprint of
Neil Wilson Publishing Ltd
303 The Pentagon Centre
36 Washington Street
GLASGOW
G3 8AZ
Tel: 0141-221-1117
Fax: 0141-221-5363

E-mail: info@nwp.co.uk
www.nwp.co.uk

ISBN 1-897784-38-4

Designed by Mark Blackadder

Printed by WS Bookwell

CONTENTS

INTRODUCTION

One of the great things about exercise, such as a hard day's walking in the hills, is that it gives you a good appetite and the excuse to indulge yourself. Although I have called this book *The Backpacker's Cookbook*, the recipes and concepts also lend themselves to cycle touring, sea kayaking and numerous other outdoor activities. If the thought of a camp meal conjures up visions of sausage and beans or a dehydrated packet of soup, think again. There is no reason why you cannot produce some exciting and appetising meals on your camp stove. With the right forethought and a few well-chosen ingredients, the possibilities are legion.

What can be better than camping out in a magnificent mountain setting, in good weather, and enjoying a gourmet meal, perhaps washed down with a glass or two of wine? You will have to choose your surroundings and take a chance on the weather, but this book will leave nothing to chance for that meal!

Since the publication of the first two editions of *The Backpacker's Cookbook* some things have changed. There have been a number of developments in stove technology and types of gas cylinder availability. I have therefore updated the first chapter to take account of this.

The other change that has occurred in the past five to ten years is the availability and choice of produce and products in the average supermarket. This may give us the advantage of being able to buy fresh fruit and vegetables all year round, but

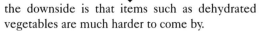

the downside is that items such as dehydrated vegetables are much harder to come by.

However, I checked with at least one major supermarket's website and managed to find all the dried products I have specified in this book. So you should either be able to find them in a large store or include them with an internet food order.

Also on the positive side is the large range of prepared meals now on offer. These meals give you plenty of convenience dishes which, while they may be a bit heavy, can be great for a short (eg weekend) trip. As an alternative, the wide range of packet sauces can be used, though the flavour and quality of these varies considerably. If you are going to use anything like this for more than a one-off, I strongly recommend trying them out before your trip.

Anyway, I hope you are not going to stick to too much of those pre-packaged items, and that is where *The Backpacker's Cookbook* comes into its own. Not all the recipes should be considered too exotic and I have included everyday dishes as well. But from time to time it is great to sample something a bit more unusual. What is more, some of the best meals need not be expensive or difficult to prepare. Careful use of seasonal local ingredients is the key here. That may mean buying ripe tomatoes, a large lettuce and fresh olives to make a simple salad in the South of France or another Mediterranean location, or perhaps you have caught a fresh trout, or picked some wild mushrooms. These simple ingredients can never be improved upon.

There are several things which set camping cookery apart and each presents its own difficulties. Each of these topics is covered with advice and techniques. The problems include: difficulty in regulating the stove, limited amount of fuel, limited number of pans, keeping food fresh and carrying food.

The biggest limitation to cooking for backpackers and campers alike is normally the type of stove used, specifically the lack of an oven and of multiple burners. Camping can vary from being on a smart campsite with the car next to you, to backpacking into the middle of nowhere, with a wide variety of situations in between. I have tried to cover the full range of backpacking and camping but some recipes are clearly more suited to one situation than another. Many of the recipes can be used just about anywhere, sometimes with a bit of adaptation. Cooking in a well-equipped caravan or at a campsite providing a comprehensive kitchen is quite common, such as in New Zealand, but has not been specifically catered for here. Obviously, if you have facilities of this sophistication you can extend your repertoire to many of the standard meals you might cook at home. Whichever path you decide to take, I hope you find the results both satisfying and rewarding.

When I first had the idea for this book I had not realized how few were the number of recipes in my regular repertoire. In carrying out my research I have acquired many more and had great fun in trying them out. Many of the recipes and ideas have originated from friends and I must thank them all, in particular Karen Beattie, Liz Briggs, Graham and Caz Dudley, Neil and Rosella Hardy, Kevin Jackson, Liz Jolley, Wendy Johnston, Dave Lecore, Eileen Lilley and Nigel Charman, Nick Nairn, Adrian Parsons, David and Barbara Pickford, Carl and Rosie Pryce, Steve Thomas and Tony Williams.

Dave Coustick
Bridge of Allan, Stirling

1

STOVES & COOKING UTENSILS

There are several types of stoves available to the backpacker and camper. Each type has good and bad points. I would say that any of the recipes can be cooked on any of the stoves, but some are easier than others. I have mentioned some of the main brand names, but these references are not comprehensive and as time goes by, names change. A whole book could be written on stoves so this is a very brief synopsis. Visit any of the manufacturers' websites for more information.

METHS-BASED STOVES

The Trangia stove is very simple, extremely stable, works well in windy conditions and is quite easy to regulate. The main problems are that it is fairly slow and uses quite a large volume of fuel. Meths can also be quite hard to get in some parts of the world.

GAS STOVES

There are many different makes and designs of gas stoves on the market, ranging from some very small ones, which make ideal backpacking stoves, to some over-elaborate devices. All are easy to use and regulate, but some can be a bit unstable and care must be taken in their use. Gas stoves also put out a high amount of heat and are great for boiling water, but with some, a concentrated flame can easily burn food if you are not careful. There are two main standards for gas cylinders, the screw-on type as used by Coleman, Go-Gas and MSR amongst others and the blue push-on type from Camping Gaz.

The best stoves use the screw-on type, but it can be difficult to get these gas cylinders in some countries. The screw-on type is much more popular in Great Britain and the USA, but Camping Gaz is still popular in many parts of Europe, especially France. The other problem with gas is that butane does not perform well in cold weather. This can be improved by using a mixture of butane and propane or, in some cases, isobutane and propane. A minimum of 20% propane is recommended and isobutane is better than butane for the remainder of the mixture. In summer it should not matter, but as temperatures drop this can become critical. Once camping in northern Norway I came across some special cartridges which were great in cold weather, although rather expensive. In winter try and keep the cartridges as warm as possible, but maybe think about using a petrol or paraffin stove (see below).

PETROL/COLEMAN FUEL STOVES

There are a number of these stoves on the market, and some will also run on paraffin (see page 9). The most common makes are Coleman,

MSR, Primus and Rekri. MSR make the Whisperlite, Dragonfly and the XGK. The latter is almost certainly the most powerful camping stove around and can burn just about any liquid fuel, but is not much good for simmering. It is absolutely ideal for the situation where the main task is to melt snow or ice for water, but as a general purpose stove I would not choose it. It is also very noisy and does not help give that wilderness experience! The Whisperlite performs well on Coleman Fuel, has a high heat output but limited regulation. The Dragonfly has good regulation and, while noisy, is one of the best (and most expensive) stoves around. Primus make a multi-fuel stove which can run on both gas and most liquid fuels, which should make it ideal for remote high-altitude expeditions. Running it on petrol tends to clog it up and it can become very fiddly to clean. Coleman fuel (white gas) has the disadvantage, at least in the UK, of being very expensive, though in the States it is much cheaper. (See appendix on page 125 for more information on fuels).

PARAFFIN STOVES

Many of the petrol stoves described above also run on paraffin with a slightly reduced heat output. Check when buying that you are getting a multi-fuel version.

The other main brands of paraffin stove are the Primus and Optimus. These were the original camping stoves and are still very effective, but are relatively big and heavy and are a bit fiddly compared to gas. The other disadvantage of paraffin is that its smell takes time to dissipate, but it is readily available worldwide.

COOKING UTENSILS

Pots and pans take up a lot of space and can be heavy, so the selection is normally quite restricted. Most recipes require one large pan for pasta/rice, etc and a second pan for the sauce or main dish. A deep frying pan is the best all-round selection for this. There is a wide range of camping cookware on the market. Aluminium is the most common choice, but this has some limitations, and is probably the most prone to burning food. Non-stick pans can be bought, though I have had a problem with some being equally non-stick on the outside. These sit happily on the stove until the contents are hot, or worse still, ready to eat, and then slide off and deposit the contents in the grass! If you are using a Trangia stove this is not a problem, as the pans sit inside the body of the stove.

Probably the best material is stainless steel, and lightweight stainless pans are now available and recommended.

Apart from the obligatory knife, fork and spoon, the only real essential is a good sharp knife, and a Swiss army knife is ideal. There are also a few other items to make things a bit easier.

A fish slice is handy for some dishes, especially for things like omelettes, fried eggs, pancakes and fish.

A teaspoon (tsp) and wooden spatula.

A small grater.

Always take a bottle opener and/or corkscrew even if you have a Swiss army knife, which serves as a good back-up. If I'm car camping I use a proper can opener, otherwise managing with the army knife.

2

CAMP COOKING

I t is worth putting together a box to carry a selection of the main staple ingredients in small quantities. Used 35mm film canisters make excellent containers for things such as salt, pepper and herbs, but remember to label them! Cooking oil needs to be in something secure such as the screw-top plastic bottles available from camping shops etc. (Make sure the type you use is suitable for fluids.) Small plastic lunch boxes are good for margarine; another possibility is to use refillable plastic tubes also available from some camping shops.

The basic staples which are required for many recipes are as follows:

Salt
Pepper
Flour (plain unless recipe states
   otherwise)
Olive or other oil
Margarine or butter
Sugar

To go with these is a selection of herbs, spices and other ingredients which can be tailored to the specific range of dishes you are going to cook. For several recipes the required combinations of herbs or spices can be assembled at home into film containers or poly bags. A basic 'starter' list is:

Mixed herbs
Oregano
Curry powder
Cinnamon (sticks preferred)

And you can also consider Jif squeezy lemon juice and a small bottle of Tabasco sauce.

As time goes by you will no doubt make your own preferred additions to this list. Margarine can become problematic (and butter even more so) in hot weather. I have included both olive oil and margarine as alternatives where the difference in the end result is not significant. However, olive oil (or other oils such as sunflower) can be used if necessary in all recipes, except for desserts, or to make a white sauce. Margarine is more versatile as it is also useful for sandwiches, bread and jam, etc. For the 'cook-at-home' recipes (see chapter 10) you may well want to use butter instead of margarine.

RECIPES

All the dishes can be cooked on two stoves at most, and many of them on a single stove. If a second stove is needed, this is clearly indicated.

Salt and pepper are not listed in individual recipes but are required (subject to taste) for virtually all dishes except desserts. Several categories of dish are described. One of these might be thought of as stretching the concept of camp cookery a little! This is dealt with in chapter 10 when food is prepared at home before the trip. You obviously could do almost anything this way, but I have included just a few recipes of things which go down particularly well out on the trail or on the hill.

Although not the norm in Britain, there are times when a camp-fire or barbecue is quite practicable and a set of recipes suitable for this style of cooking are also included (see chapter 11). Certainly most camping sites in the USA and Australia are equipped with barbecues as a standard feature.

QUANTITIES

A 'spoon' means a dessertspoon, this being the typical camping utensil. A level spoonful is assumed unless stated otherwise. A teaspoon (tsp) is also used as a measure for items such as spices.

For rice and pulses I have quoted weights in grams (g) and ounces (oz), but a coffee mug is an easy way to measure when out on the trail. However, since mugs vary considerably by a factor of up to three times, it's important to take this into account. Check how your own mug measures up so you can use it correctly. Some of the quantities may seem precise, but they have been based on standard sizes generally available in shops.

The recipes are all based on quantities for two people, except for some of the 'cook-at-home' cakes and the like. If you're on your own it should be easy to divide by two. For larger numbers the usual problem is that the pans are not big enough, so it is often easier to cook two separate sets of food if there are four of you.

While the recipes are intended to provide reasonable portions for two after a day in the hills, you may want to increase the amount of rice or pasta if you are a big eater, or if you are on an extended trip. Even allowing for a reasonable breakfast, a typical sandwich lunch and a snack of chocolate bars, the portions given are unlikely to meet up with the energy consumed on a long day out. If you calculate the number of calories consumed on a typical day in the hills, taking in a couple of Munros with 1500m (4920ft) of ascent, the total is between 5-6000! This is not an especially long day, and if you go for an even more epic walk, it is quite possible to get through 8000 calories in a day. These figures are based on the information in *Mountaincraft and Leadership* by Eric Langmuir. (See also the expedition menus in chapter 3).

For a weekend, many people tend not to eat the number of calories likely to be burnt off. However if you are on a week-long backpacking trip it becomes much more important to balance input and output, so be prepared to carry extra pasta, rice, etc.

KEEPING FOOD FRESH

Camping is obviously more popular in the summer and many of us go off to seek a sunny area. Unfortunately, this is not ideal for keeping fresh food at its best, but there are one or two things which can be done to help.

If you are car-camping, it is well worth investing in a cold-box. I found that even when flying to the United States and renting a car it was well worth investing in one. The cost is soon recouped in the lack of wasted food, plus the improved taste of ingredients. In the United States bags of ice are readily available at gas stations, motels and truck stops, while in most European countries cold packs can be put in a freezer overnight at many campsites.

Another useful technique, especially for keeping that chilled bottle of wine cold during your walk, is to put it inside your (packed) sleeping bag, which will keep it cool for several hours. It is also relatively easy to make an effective refrigerator by soaking a towel or a T-shirt in water then wrapping this around the item to be cooled. Leave this in the sun. The evaporation is very effective in chilling the item, but be aware that as soon as the towel dries out the 'fridge' turns instantly into an oven, so keep an eye on it and be ready to re-soak as required.

There are also a few general points about packing and storing food. For liquids such as fresh milk and wine, I tend to use the metal Sigg bottles to avoid the danger of leakage or breakage in the rucksack. There is nothing worse than finding all your kit is impregnated with red wine! If you have things in polythene bags, make sure they are well-labelled. Powdered milk, flour and instant mashed potato all look remarkably similar, but use of the wrong ingredient can ruin an otherwise well-prepared meal.

Watch out for vermin. If this is expected to be a problem where you are camped then make sure food is well out the way inside a rucksack or in the tent. However, this does not apply if you are in bear country. In this case, you must never have food in the tent. In this situation take note of the recommendations from the locals; basically, food should be hidden in an inaccessible place.

NATURE'S LARDER

There are plenty of opportunities to gather food while you are out in the countryside. I am certainly not going into the snaring of rabbits or the like, but the possibility of catching fish is more realistic. Collecting shellfish, such as mussels, along the seashore at low tide is a distinct possibility, providing the area is known to be pollution-free; regrettably this constraint seems to be a growing problem. But the main source of food in the wild for most people is the odd handful of blackberries, or some wonderful mushrooms. There are quite a few fruits which are more or less common depending on where you are. Apart from the blackberries mentioned above, one can reasonably expect to find bilberries (also known as blaeberries or blueberries), wild raspberries and occasionally cloudberries. The latter are common in Scandinavia, but in Britain you will be lucky to get enough to make a meal. Cloudberries grow on a small plant in high hill country and produce only a single fruit on each plant, unusually turning from red (unripe) to yellow (ripe).

Mushrooms and other members of the fungus family are well-established as a source of free food, but it is essential that you are able to identify the mushrooms in question. The golden rule has to be: if in doubt, leave it out.

It is not the intention of this book to cover either mushroom identification or indeed the possibilities of many other plants that can be used. What I have done is to include a few recipes where the use of such ingredients can at least enhance and, in some cases, actually make the dish. If you want to explore this area more, I recommend you get a book specifically on the topic, such as *Food for Free* by Richard Mabey.

SHORT CUTS

There are a number of shortcuts that might not be considered good technique in the kitchen at home, but when backpacking become invaluable. These are ways of saving time, fuel and/or weight.

Instead of using cream, make up powdered milk to twice the strength given on the packet.

In order to save both time and the need for an extra stove when cooking pasta, use the technique described in chapter 5.

Although fresh vegetables are listed in many of the recipes, it is usually possible to substitute dried vegetables for these, and most do not take too long to reconstitute; normally 20-30 minutes steeped in cold water is enough. Not all are easy to get, but if you know a good Italian delicatessen this should be a good source for sun-dried tomatoes and various dried mushrooms. Other sources are health food stores or shops specialising in loose ingredients in bins.

3

EXPEDITION MENUS FOR 7 DAYS

Here is a selection of menus to provide for a week-long backpacking trip or other expedition. For this reason they are based on the use of a large proportion of dried ingredients. Obviously you can chop and change or substitute any part of these menus. For example I tend to have muesli for breakfast every day but I know plenty of people who prefer porridge. Using the quantities indicated in the recipes the daily calorie intake is shown on the right hand side. Although the recipes are designed for two people, the quantities listed in these menus are given per person, as it is easier to assess, adjust quantities and pack on this basis. The menus include the use of packet soups (a 1-litre or 1¼-pint packet between two) and proprietary items such as Angel Delight. Tea, coffee or other drinks are not listed but I normally allow for five to six mugs a day. If you take sugar, each teaspoonful adds 25 calories.

DAY 1

Breakfast	Calories
75g/3oz muesli with 5 dried apricots & 575ml/20fl oz milk	380
3 slices bread with margarine & jam/honey	430
Mid morning	
115g/4oz marzipan	440

Lunch

Salami sandwiches (4 slices bread, 55g/2oz salami)	700
1 flapjack	300

Afternoon

1 chocolate bar (115g/4oz)	500

Dinner

Chicken soup	200
Dried vegetable pasta (see page 39)	550
Ground rice pudding (see page 94)	140

TOTAL	3640

DAY 2

Breakfast

3 Weetabix with 30g/1oz raisins & 575ml/20fl oz milk & 1 spoon sugar	325
3 slices bread with margarine & jam/honey	430

Mid morning

115g/4oz raisins	250

Lunch

Cheese sandwiches (4 slices bread, 55g/2oz cheese)	640
4 biscuits	240

Afternoon

1 chocolate bar (115g/4oz)	500

Dinner

Lentil soup	160
Tuna pasta (see page 48)	800
Angel Delight	190

TOTAL	3535

DAY 3

Breakfast

Porridge made from 55g/2oz oatmeal, 100ml/4fl oz milk & 1 spoon sugar	365
3 slices bread with margarine & jam/honey	430

Mid morning

1 sunflower bar	300

Lunch

Salami sandwiches (4 slices bread, 55g/2oz salami)	700
115g/4oz raisins	250

Afternoon

1 chocolate bar (115g/4oz)	500

Dinner

Mushroom soup	180
Soya mince cottage pie (see page 84)	630
Dried apricots (115g/4oz)	185

TOTAL	**3540**

DAY 4

Breakfast

75g/3oz muesli with 5 dried apricots & 575ml/20fl oz milk	380
3 slices bread with margarine & jam/honey	430

Mid morning

75g/3oz peanuts	440

Lunch

Bulgur wheat with tomato & pepper (see page 24)	340

1 flapjack	300
Afternoon	
1 chocolate bar (115g/4oz)	500
Dinner	
Tomato soup	180
Four cheese pasta (see page 38)	750
Stewed dried fruit (115g/4oz before reconstituting)	
with instant custard	200
TOTAL	**3520**

DAY 5

Breakfast	
3 Weetabix with 30g/1oz raisins, 575ml/20fl oz milk &	
1 spoon sugar	325
3 slices bread with margarine &	
jam/honey	430
Mid morning	
115g/4oz marzipan	440
Lunch	
Salami sandwiches (4 slices bread,	
55g/2oz salami)	700
115g/4oz raisins	250
Afternoon	
1 chocolate bar (115g/4oz)	500
Dinner	
Chicken soup	190
Risotto (see page 60)	470
Pancakes with jam/honey	
(see page 95)	300
TOTAL	**3605**

DAY 6

Breakfast
75g/3oz muesli with 5 dried
   apricots & 575ml/20fl oz milk   380
3 slices bread with margarine &
   jam/honey   430

Mid morning
115g/4oz marzipan   440

Lunch
Salami (55g/2oz) with
   pumpernickel (4 slices)   600
55g/2oz peanuts   300

Afternoon
1 chocolate bar (115g/4oz)   500

Dinner
Tomato soup   180
Lentil and mushroom casserole
   (see page 55)   680
Angel Delight   190

TOTAL   3700

DAY 7

Breakfast
3 Weetabix with 30g/1oz raisins,
   575ml/20fl oz milk &
   1 spoon sugar   325
3 slices bread with margarine &
   jam/honey   430

Mid morning
55g/2oz peanuts   300

Lunch

Cheese (55g/2oz) with pumpernickel (4 slices)	540
1 sunflower bar	300

Afternoon

1 chocolate bar (115g/4oz)	500

Dinner

Vegetable soup	190
Pasta with tomato sauce (see page 44)	580
Dried apple & instant custard	200
TOTAL	**3365**

4

STARTERS, LUNCHES, SALADS & VEGETABLES

Although many people consider starters rather a luxury when camping, it's often nice to have something extra, and something which is made quickly while waiting for the main course. Soups are a favourite but there are also quite a few interesting alternatives. Many dishes can also be used for lunch as a change from the ubiquitous sandwich. They can either be prepared the night before or when you stop, especially if you're having a leisurely day. If you decide to make the dish the night before, simply double up on your starter quantities. Another thing you can do is use some leftover pasta sauce as a sandwich filling.

Soups are generally best made from packets since using fresh ingredients takes a long time, and using dried ingredients has little benefit compared to a packet soup. However there are a few ways you can improve or spice up these packet items.

Mushroom, chicken: add a few fresh mushrooms for the last couple of minutes of cooking.

Vegetable, tomato: add some dried herbs or chopped fresh vegetables as soon as the water is boiling; or add fresh herbs or a dash of Tabasco just before serving.

For vegetables there are of course many standard types which can be used according to taste and availability. What I've tried to do is to include a few ideas beyond the simple boiled versions.

As mentioned at the end of chapter two, dried vegetables are a useful item for carrying on a longer trip, but only in a few cases do these come out well enough to be served separately.

Salads are great when car-camping in hot weather. When you are in areas such as the Mediterranean the choice of fresh, succulent ingredients is enormous and a salad makes a great starter or accompaniment. When it's really hot, a salad is sufficient on its own if accompanied with fresh bread, and a glass of chilled rosé wine.

BULGUR WHEAT WITH TOMATO & PEPPER

Bulgur wheat is a good form of carbohydrate for camping as it requires minimal cooking. In this salad recipe it is used cold but it can also be used hot instead of rice, pasta or potatoes. The following recipe makes a good lunch dish, or can be used to supplement a main course. I realised this when camped alongside the Colorado River in Utah, near the trendy town of Moab. Unusual and dramatic desert scenery surrounds the town which has become a mecca for mountain-biking and includes the famous 'Slick Rock Trail'.

1 large tomato, chopped
1 green pepper, seeded and chopped
225g/8oz bulgur wheat
1 tsp chopped mint (optional)

Add boiling salted water to the bulgur wheat and let it stand for about 15 minutes; drain and allow to cool a little. Then simply add the tomato, pepper and mint (if using) and mix well.

Variation
Other vegetables can be added, such as courgette, carrot or anything else you like.

If you are basing this dish on dried vegetables, then sun-dried tomatoes and freeze-dried peas are a good combination.

GARLIC MUSHROOMS

This is the easiest and tastiest of starters, as long as you like garlic mushrooms of course! I first used this when camping in Glen Coe on a typically wet weekend. We had just finished a long traverse over the Black Mount from Victoria Bridge; we had hoped to ski nearly all of it but spent most of the time carrying the skis! We were very hungry and rather than wait for our main course we extracted the mushrooms and cooked them separately to get something hot inside us. Garlic mushrooms have stayed on the regular menu ever since.

140g/5oz mushrooms
2 cloves garlic, peeled and chopped
3 spoons margarine or olive oil

Chop the garlic finely and fry gently for a couple of minutes in the margarine or oil. I prefer margarine, or better still, butter, since it gives a better flavour, but if you want to be healthier in your eating, stick to olive oil. While this is frying, chop the mushrooms into quarters, or slice them, and add to the pan. Cook for a further three to five minutes until the mushrooms are soft. Serve with fresh bread or on their own.

Variation
Add some chopped parsley or a few mixed herbs to give variety and a touch of colour.

GUACAMOLE

Thanks go to Caz Dudley for this simple dip to have with your tortilla chips, while waiting for the chilli con carne (see page 52) to cook. The most memorable location for this dish was when I was in the Rocky Mountains National Park in the north of Colorado, walking amongst the magnificent pines and lakes. Being July most of the trails should have been open but after a more severe winter than usual, many were still blocked. However this meant the scenery was even more dramatic, and helped encourage the wildlife to come down to the lower levels.

2 ripe avocados
2 cloves garlic, peeled and chopped finely
½ to 1 tsp chilli powder
Juice of 1 lemon (or use a squeezy lemon)
140g/5oz tub sour cream (optional)

Cut the avocados in half and scoop out the flesh into a bowl or pan; mash with a fork. Add the garlic with the chilli powder and lemon juice and mix well. To make it creamier, add the sour cream.

MACKEREL PÂTÉ

A simple starter first tasted in a hut in southern Norway on a November weekend of walking. We had perfect weather with blue skies and much of the ground was frozen crisp. We made a circuit of Store Auravatnet staying overnight at Litle Aurådal. This provided me with some magnificent photographs, with the patterns in the ice offsetting the rocks jutting out from the streams.

200g/7oz smoked mackerel
2 spoons horseradish sauce
Half a small tub of sour cream (140g/5oz)
Juice of half a lemon (optional)

Mash up the mackerel with the horseradish and mix in the sour cream and lemon juice. You now have instant and delicious pâté. Serve on biscuits or bread, and if you have some left over, it's perfect for tomorrow's lunch.

PRAWN SALAD

This salad ideally needs large prawns, not the ones you normally see in British supermarkets. We purchased superb prawns at the small town of Buis-les-Baronnies in Southern France. Originally planned for a sauce to have with our fish, the prawns were too good for that and hence this salad was created. Buis-les-Baronnies is an old town with an impressive looking limestone fin on a nearby hillside providing good rock-climbing. There is also plenty of interesting walking in the area.

8 large prawns (adjust number dependent on their size and your appetite)
1 medium tomato
A few lettuce leaves
Half a green pepper, seeded
2 spoons olive oil
1 spoon lemon juice

There's not really much to this recipe — you just make the salad as simple or as sophisticated as you wish. Wash the lettuce, slice the tomato and pepper and arrange on the plate with the prawns, still in their shells. To make the dressing, which is optional, simply mix the olive oil and lemon juice plus a little salt and pepper and whisk in a mug or glass. I use lemon juice rather than vinegar partly for personal preference, but it's also easier to buy a small quantity of lemon juice (i.e. one lemon).

RATATOUILLE

One of the classic vegetable dishes and very adaptable in terms of ingredients. Olive oil, tomatoes and peppers are the base but beyond that there is quite a choice. Of course it has to be reminiscent of Southern France — this time the Queyras. This region, not well-known outside France, lies in the South-east of the country, a couple of hours drive north of Marseilles. The mountains are not huge but this is a brilliant area for walking and gentle ski-touring. Views extend to Monte Viso in Italy, which is just under 4000m/13,130ft but was once thought to be the highest peak in the Alps.

1 medium onion, peeled and sliced
1 clove garlic, peeled and chopped
1 x 225g/8oz tin tomatoes or 3 fresh
    plum tomatoes
1 red pepper and 1 green pepper, seeded
    and sliced into long, thin strips
2 small courgettes, sliced
2 spoons olive oil

Fry the onion and garlic in the oil until soft but not brown. Add the peppers to the onions and fry gently for a few minutes. Then add courgettes and tomatoes if fresh; if tinned tomatoes are used let the courgettes cook for a few minutes before the tomatoes, without their juice, are added. Season and simmer very gently for ten minutes.

RÖSTI

This one I first tasted well away from camping, on a mountaineering trip to Switzerland. The region I visited was around Andermatt where ski-mountaineering is a popular activity. Rösti makes a fine supplement to liver or barbecued/fried chops, or try it on a cold winter morning as a breakfast dish.

450g/1lb potatoes
55g/2oz Cheddar or Gruyère cheese

**1 large onion, peeled and chopped
   (optional)**
3 spoons margarine or olive oil

Par-boil the potatoes for about ten minutes so
that they are still firm. Ideally this can be done in
advance so they have cooled down before the
next stage. Cut them into very fine strips, as near
to grating as you can manage. Mix with the
cheese, either grated or finely chopped and the
onion; then season the mixture. Heat the
margarine or oil in a frying-pan and when hot put
in the potato mixture, pushing down with a fork
or fish slice to flatten. Turn from time to time
until golden-brown.

Variation
Add some chopped ham, double the quantity
of cheese and add an egg (or top with a fried egg)
and this becomes a full meal.

SALAD NIÇOISE

This could be more than just a starter,
depending on how much extra you throw in. It is
naturally associated with the town of Nice in
Southern France. The spectacular Verdon Gorge
nearby is, I believe, the deepest in Europe at
300m/984ft. The climbing is awesome, but none
too easy as I discovered on being hauled up one
of the so-called easier routes. There is also a
pleasant day-walk along the bottom of the gorge
but take a headtorch for the tunnel!

200g/7oz can of tuna
1 or 2 eggs
Half a lettuce
**1 small Spanish onion, or a few spring
   onions**
1 tomato, sliced
115g/4oz fresh olives
Olive oil to taste (see text)

Hard-boil the egg(s) far enough in advance to let them cool. Wash the lettuce and lay this as the base of the salad. Peeled and slice the onion thinly, or chop the spring onions; add these on top of the lettuce. Then add sliced tomato and the hard-boiled egg(s), either sliced or quartered and top with the fish. If the tuna is in olive oil this can be used to sprinkle over the salad; if in brine then drain and use fresh olive oil. Scatter the olives (fresh olives are so much better than tinned or packet). You can use green or black or a mixture depending on your preference. Serve with fresh French bread, wine and sunshine.

Variation
Replace tuna with anchovies and/or add some chopped nuts.

SARDINE SALAD

If fresh sardines are available, as they are likely to be, for example, in Portugal, they can be quickly fried and used in place of the tinned type. It was actually a tin of sardines I used on the West Indian island of Canouan. I was taking a few days island-hopping by boat and walking on some of the Windward Islands. Of these it is Union Island which is the most dramatic and the views of this from the boat at sunset, were spectacular.

120g tin of sardines in oil
1 tomato
1 green pepper, seeded and sliced
1 carrot, sliced into thin strips
Juice of half a lemon (optional)

Slice the tomato and arrange with the pepper and carrot. Drain the oil from the sardines and mix with the lemon juice and pour over the salad items. If not using lemon juice just pour the oil. Arrange the sardines next to the salad and add salt and pepper to taste.

Variation
Vary the salad items according to availability.

SAUTÉ POTATOES

Sauté potatoes make a change from mash and go well with omelettes if you have a second stove, or with any of the barbecue dishes. They can also be a good for breakfast or on their own as a late night snack after an evening walk or cycle. Glen Tilt in Perthshire is perfect for this type of activity. This glen is surrounded by plenty of Munros, some relatively remote, so the area cries out for weekend or longer expeditions. A good way to visit the area is to cycle from Braemar to Blair Atholl, taking in the adjacent peaks on foot, and swap car keys with like-minded friends at the other end. The road journey round is a long, long way!

450g/1lb potatoes
2 spoons margarine
1 spoon chopped parsley (optional)

Boil the potatoes for about ten minutes in salted water. Drain and slice. Melt the margarine and when hot add the potatoes and fry for a few minutes on each side; sprinkle with chopped parsley.

Variation
A little chopped bacon can be added when you start frying. You can also make things really easy by buying the ready cooked product available in foil packets from good supermarkets and simply reheat.

STIR-FRIED VEGETABLES

Stir-frying is a quick and simple way to prepare vegetables; the fresher they are the tastier this dish is. A local climb is ideal for this dish, such as Lochnagar (1155m/3789ft) near Aberdeen. There is no problem carrying in the fresh ingredients since a short walk will bring you to some pleasant camping spots with good views of Lochnagar and some of the other hills in the area.

> 1 large onion, peeled and sliced
> 2 cloves garlic, peeled and chopped
> 1 red pepper, seeded and sliced
> 1 green pepper, seeded and sliced
> 2 medium carrots, sliced and cut into thin strips
> 1 courgette, sliced
> 2 medium tomatoes, quartered
> 3 spoons olive oil
> 1 tsp oregano

Fry the onion and garlic in the oil until soft but not brown. Add the carrot and fry for a couple of minutes more. Then add the courgette, peppers and oregano; fry for another two minutes. Finally add the tomatoes; I normally cut these into quarters rather than slices. Continue cooking until the tomatoes begin to break up slightly; season to taste. Serve with rice, or use a smaller quantity to supplement a main dish.

Variation

Almost any vegetable can be added. You can also include thin strips of meat such as beef; in this case add the meat before the carrot and fry for a couple of minutes on each side.

TOMATO SALAD

Another recipe for the sunshine, and in this case it was that magic warm sunshine that sometimes comes to North-west Scotland. I was making a circuit of the 'Fisherfield Six', one of the best walks there is if you are as lucky as I was with the weather. Making the approach on the

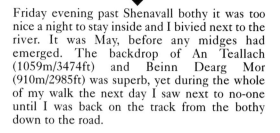

Friday evening past Shenavall bothy it was too nice a night to stay inside and I bivied next to the river. It was May, before any midges had emerged. The backdrop of An Teallach (1059m/3474ft) and Beinn Dearg Mor (910m/2985ft) was superb, yet during the whole of my walk the next day I saw next to no-one until I was back on the track from the bothy down to the road.

> 2 large tomatoes
> A few spring onions
> 1 spoon chopped parsley
> 1 or 2 spoons olive oil
> Juice of half a lemon (optional)

Slice the tomatoes. Peel and chop the spring onions and scatter them over the tomatoes. Either pour the oil over the tomatoes or mix the oil and lemon juice to form a simple dressing. Sprinkle with chopped parsley. A simple salad such as this can accompany a dehydrated meal and turn it from being merely necessary fuel into an enjoyable dinner.

5

PASTA DISHES

Pasta must be one of the most suitable items for camp cooking. It is easy to carry, easy to cook and is good nutritionally, being full of carbohydrate. I have suggested certain shapes of pasta for particular dishes but you can ring the changes here. Spaghetti is not quite as easy to cook in a small pan, although it does pack well, so I tend to stick to bows, twists and tubes; the tagliatelle nests are also quite easy to cook. Shell-shaped pasta is trickier to drain without a colander so it is best left at home.

Although ideally pasta should be cooked in a large pot at a rolling boil it is quite possible to use some camping short cuts. A small pan should present no problem, subject to the comments above, but do not put too much pasta in as it expands considerably. A pan with one litre of water is okay for 255g/9oz of pasta. To cook, bring the salted water to the boil with a dash of oil added (optional) and add the pasta, giving a good stir and boil for about a minute. After this you can take it off the stove and the pasta will continue to cook while you use the stove to prepare your sauce in another pan. A couple of times during the cooking return the pasta pan to the stove and bring back it to the boil for ten to 15 seconds. The overall cooking time by this method will be a little longer than the manufacturer suggests, but normally the pasta will be ready when the sauce is cooked.

Some people prefer wholemeal pasta but this does take longer to cook.

Parmesan has been included with most dishes. While not essential in all recipes, it does liven up most pasta sauces and is easy to carry. Packets of grated parmesan are readily available at most supermarkets and because quantity is not that critical you can just take along a small packet. If you are carrying a small grater, then it makes sense to also keep a lump of fresh parmesan handy. It will keep fairly well and is much tastier.

BROCCOLI & CAULIFLOWER PASTA

I recall preparing this the evening before a mountain marathon. This event was held in the Arrochar Alps in Argyll. Although less than an hour's drive north-west of Glasgow, it is a little frequented area and well worth a visit. For such an area of rugged terrain this was an ideal, substantial dish giving plenty of energy. On that occasion we ate it accompanied by garlic mushrooms which complements it well.

140g/5oz broccoli in small heads
140g/5oz cauliflower (about half a small one)
1 medium onion, peeled and chopped
1 clove garlic, peeled and chopped
30g/1oz cheese (Cheddar or Double Gloucester)
300ml/½pt milk
2 spoons olive oil
1 spoon margarine
1 heaped spoon flour
1 spoon mixed herbs
255g/9oz pasta bows
30g/1oz parmesan (optional)

Cook pasta as described on page 34.
Fry the onion and garlic in the oil until soft but not brown. Meanwhile chop the broccoli and cauliflower into small pieces; add these to the

onion and fry gently for a few minutes more. Add
the margarine and as soon as this has melted add
the flour, stirring until it is well mixed in.
Gradually add milk, stirring continuously to form
a sauce. Add herbs and salt and pepper to season.
Cook gently for two minutes and then add
cheese in small pieces allowing this to melt into
the sauce.

After serving sprinkle with parmesan if
desired.

Variation
Before adding the flour add a small (115g/4oz)
tin of tuna.

PASTA ARRABIATA

'Fiery Pasta' is the meaning of this recipe's
name; it came to me from friends at the tranquil
location of Ax-les-Thermes. This small town
nestles in the Pyrénées not far from Andorra.
This is a wonderful area for walking, mountain
biking and cross-country skiing with beautiful
woods covering most of the hills up to
1500m/4923ft or so. At the end of the day you can
sit in the town square and soak your tired feet in
the hot thermal waters.

> 1 x 400g/14oz tin plum tomatoes
>   (chopped or whole)
> 6 cloves garlic, peeled and chopped
> 1 fistful of parsley, chopped
> 2 dried red chillies, with seeds, chopped
> 3 spoons olive oil
> 255g/9oz penne

Cook pasta as described on page 34.
Fry garlic and chillies lightly in the oil until
soft but not brown. Add the tomatoes to the pan;
if whole, chop them before adding. Heat through
thoroughly while mixing well. Remove from the
heat, add in the parsley and pour the mixture

over the pasta. Mix pasta and sauce well and this simple dish is ready.

CHICKEN, HAM & CREAM

One of the more luxurious dishes which I have included. The richness of this matches the richness of the scenery in Glen Affric, lying to the west of Inverness. This contains one of the few remaining areas of Caledonian pine forest which is a magnificent complement to the Scottish hill scenery and together they provide a landscape unequalled anywhere. It is to be regretted that so many of these indigenous forests have been destroyed, but perhaps with the more informed thinking which is now prevalent, regeneration over the coming years will help re-establish these native woodlands.

200g/7oz chicken meat, breast preferred (boneless)
55g/2oz cooked ham (chopped)
1 small onion, peeled and chopped
1 clove garlic, peeled and chopped
100ml/4fl oz dry white wine
100ml/4fl oz cream
3 spoons olive oil or margarine
1 tsp oregano or tarragon
255g/9oz tagliatelle

Cook the pasta as described on page 34.

Fry the onion and garlic in one spoonful of oil or margarine until soft but not brown. Slice chicken into thin strips. Increase the heat and ensure that the oil is hot before adding chicken strips and stir well for a few minutes until cooked through. Add the wine together with the ham and herbs; cook gently until the wine has reduced by half and then stir in the cream and cook for a further minute. Season to taste.

Variation

A few mushrooms can be incorporated; chop and add at the same time as the ham.

If cream is not convenient you can coat the chicken in flour and replace the cream with milk to make a white sauce; for this variant margarine is preferable to olive oil.

FOUR CHEESE PASTA

This is, I believe, a classic Italian recipe, but I came across it in France while camping next to some Italians at the mountain village of La Berade in the Dauphiné Alps (Parc National des Ecrins). This is a great centre for walking, climbing and ski-touring and is sufficiently isolated to remain unspoilt. Generally the road in is closed during the winter months which helps to retain its character.

30g/1oz gruyère cheese
30g/1oz fontina (or edam) cheese
30g/1oz gorgonzola cheese
30g/1oz parmesan cheese
30g/1oz butter or margarine
75ml/3fl oz milk or cream
255g/9oz pasta bows or tubes

Cook the pasta as described on page 34.

This is one recipe where I have listed butter as this is to be preferred, but margarine will do. Although I've called this Four Cheese Pasta you can get away with fewer varieties. The types of cheese to use can be adjusted according to availability.

Warm the milk or cream and butter. Cut the cheese into pieces and gradually add these in. Season with plenty of black pepper and stir in the pasta, mixing well before serving.

FRESH VEGETABLES WITH PASTA TWIRLS

As I had just completed a circuit of quite a few of the Mamores, with well over 2000m/6560ft of ascent, I was ready for this meal. My tent was at Steall Bridge, a beautiful spot nestling at the top end of Glen Nevis and a perfect base for many Munros, with several opportunities for marvellous walking.

1 large or 2 medium onions, peeled and chopped
1 large or 2 medium carrots, sliced
1 clove garlic, peeled and chopped
115g/4oz mushrooms, sliced or chopped
140g/5oz broccoli in small heads
1 courgette, sliced
1 green pepper, seeded and chopped
1 x 400g/14oz can tomatoes
1 tsp oregano
2 spoons olive oil or margarine
255g/9oz pasta twirls
30g/1oz parmesan (optional)

Cook pasta as described on page 34.

Fry the onion and garlic in the oil or margarine for a couple of minutes and then add the carrots; continue to cook until the onion is soft but not brown. Add the courgette, mushrooms, pepper and fry for a few minutes more. Add the small heads of broccoli together with the oregano, tomatoes and seasoning. Bring to the boil and simmer gently for ten minutes.

After serving with the pasta, sprinkle with parmesan if desired.

DRIED VEGETABLE PASTA

This is rather different from the recipe with fresh vegetables. Although not as tasty it is only about a quarter of the weight, including the pasta, so it is a good one to take on a long trip, perhaps as a contingency meal. This does need the parmesan, or some other cheese to give it the extra flavour. I carried this when I was making a multi-day trip along the Rees-Dart Track in New Zealand during early spring. The walk provided a few challenges but I was rewarded with fantastic views, clear frosty days and a peace unobtainable on such a popular route in summer.

> **2 cloves garlic, peeled and chopped**
> **55g/2oz dried onions**
> **1 small packet (115g/4oz) freeze-dried peas**
> **30g/1oz dried mushrooms**
> **Quarter of 125g/4½oz tube tomato purée**
> **1 tsp dried mixed herbs**
> **1 spoon olive oil or margarine**
> **255g/9oz pasta tubes**
> **30g/1oz parmesan**

About 20 to 30 minutes before starting the cooking, soak the onions and tomatoes in about 300ml/½pt water.

Cook pasta as described on page 34 .

Fry the garlic in oil or margarine for a couple of minutes. Add the onions and mushrooms (including the water in which they were soaked), herbs and seasoning. Mix in tomato purée well and cook for a couple of minutes. Add the freeze-dried peas, return to the boil for another two to three minutes and then remove from heat; add a little water if necessary to give the right consistency. Let it stand for a few minutes before serving, and then sprinkle with parmesan.

MACARONI WITH BROCCOLI & SMOKED SALMON

A development from Macaroni Cheese which changes it into a luxury dish, worthy for any occasion. One such was after a long foggy drive from London when we arrived at Capel Curig to a cold night where even the taps were frozen at the campsite. The following day a traverse of the Snowdon Horseshoe in perfect winter conditions must be the best day out I've experienced in Wales.

200g/7oz broccoli florets
55-115g/2-4oz smoked salmon
30g/1oz margarine
30g/1oz flour
55g/2oz cheddar cheese, grated or chopped
300ml/½pt milk
255g/9oz macaroni, or other pasta

Cook the macaroni as described on page 34.

Cook the broccoli florets with the pasta and remove them when ready (after a few minutes) when they float to the surface. Cut the smoked salmon into small strips.

Melt the margarine and add the flour, stirring until well mixed, then cook gently for a minute before gradually adding the milk, stirring continuously to make a thick sauce; season to taste. Add the cheese and mix well. Once all the cheese has melted and the sauce is smooth, add the broccoli and smoked salmon. Cook for a minute or two more and pour over the macaroni.

Variation
To cut down on weight you can omit the broccoli, perhaps substituting with some freeze-dried peas.

MUSHROOM & HERB PASTA

If you are lucky enough to come across wild mushrooms of any sort, these make an ideal ingredient for this. I prepared this for the first time near Schiehallion, the shapely Perthshire mountain which looks at its most impressive when viewed from the west across Rannoch Moor. After eating the dish I climbed the hill as dusk approached to view a great Scottish sunset.

15g/½oz dried porcini mushrooms
140g/5oz fresh mushrooms, sliced, wild if available,
1 clove garlic, peeled and chopped
150ml/¼pt dry white wine
75ml/3fl oz cream
1 tsp dried or 2 spoons chopped fresh herbs (oregano or sage preferred)
2 shallots or 1 small onion, peeled and chopped
1 spoon olive oil
255g/9oz tagliatelle
30g/1oz parmesan (ungrated if possible)

Cook pasta as described on page 34.

Soak the porcini mushrooms for about 20 minutes in a little boiled water. Fry the garlic and onion or shallots lightly in the oil until soft but not brown. Add the dried mushrooms (together with the liquid in which they were soaked) plus the wine and the herbs (if dried are used). Cook over a reasonably strong heat until the liquid has reduced by about half and then add the fresh mushrooms and cook for a couple of minutes more. Stir in the cream, (and fresh herbs if used), season to taste and cook very gently.

Pour over the pasta and top with thin shavings of parmesan.

PASTA BOLOGNAISE

'Spag Bol' must be many people's first introduction to pasta. Although a regular recipe at home, it was some time into my outdoor experience before I used it. It is another reminder of the South Island of New Zealand as I walked up the Matukituki valley which is a typical braided river with omnipresent rainforest on either side. Spectacular mountains surround it with names such as Rob Roy Peak and Mount Avalanche as well as many with Maori names — there is even a Mount Maori!

255g/9oz minced beef
115g/4oz mushrooms, sliced
1 x 400g/14oz tin tomatoes
1 large onion, peeled and chopped
1 clove garlic, peeled and chopped
1 tsp oregano
2 spoons olive oil or margarine
255g/9oz pasta bows
30g/1oz parmesan (optional)

Cook pasta as described on page 34.

Fry the onion and garlic in the oil or margarine until soft but not brown. Add the mince and keep stirring well to prevent burning. Once the meat has browned, cook for a few minutes and then add the mushrooms. Cook and stir for a couple of minutes more before adding the tomatoes, salt, pepper and oregano. Bring to the boil and simmer for ten to 15 minutes.

Pour over the pasta and sprinkle with parmesan if desired.

Variation

To save weight replace the tinned tomatoes with half a small tube of tomato purée; a little water should then be added to stop the sauce sticking.

This dish can also be made with 200g/7oz soya mince. In this case add the mushrooms and oregano once the onion has softened. Then add water of 1½ times the volume of mince after the mushrooms have cooked and add the mince once the water has boiled. Then add tomatoes and seasoning; once brought back to the boil it is ready.

PASTA CARBONARA

This is not quite the classic recipe for pasta carbonara as this does not use eggs, since these are obviously awkward to carry. Although not a substantial sauce it is quite rich and to my mind imparts a good warmth to a damp autumn day such as the one I spent in the hills just north of Fort William. The peaks of Streap (909m/2982ft) and Braigh nan Uamhachan (765m/2510ft) provide a wonderful outlook over Glenfinnan to Loch Shiel; unfortunately the area suffers a lot from the west coast precipitation.

- **115g/4oz bacon, preferably streaky, chopped**
- **2 cloves garlic, peeled and chopped**
- **75ml/3fl oz dry white wine (or stock if wine is not available)**
- **75ml/3fl oz single cream**
- **1 tsp oregano (or 1 spoon fresh parsley if available)**
- **1 spoon olive oil or margarine**
- **45g/1½oz parmesan or half parmesan and half cheddar (grated)**
- **255g/9oz penne (pasta tubes)**

Cook pasta as described on page 34.

Fry the garlic gently in the oil or margarine for a few minutes, then add the bacon and fry for about five minutes until almost crisp. Drain off most of the surplus fat, add the wine and cook gently until reduced by half. Stir in the cream and oregano or parsley and half the cheese. If using a mixture of cheeses, add the cheddar first; this does not need to be grated if you find it easier just to slice it. Cook for a couple of minutes more, season to taste and pour over the pasta. Sprinkle with the remaining parmesan.

Serve on its own or perhaps with some ratatouille (see page 28.)

PASTA WITH TOMATO SAUCE

Another simple and lightweight recipe. I've used this one on a mountain marathon in the Lake District where we camped in a pleasant but cold spot near Langdale. Despite the crowds this remains a beautiful area and if you avoid the busiest times it retains that unique Lake District quality.

> **2 cloves garlic, peeled and chopped**
> **30g/1oz dried onions or mixed vegetables**
> **Half a 125g/4½oz tube tomato purée**
> **4 sun-dried tomatoes, chopped**
> **1 tsp oregano**
> **1 spoon oil or margarine**
> **255g/9oz pasta twirls**
> **45g/1½oz parmesan (optional)**

About 20 to 30 minutes before starting, soak the dried onions and sun-dried tomatoes in 300ml/½pt water.

Cook pasta as described on page 34.

Fry the garlic in oil or margarine for a couple of minutes. Add the onions and tomatoes (including the water in which they were soaked), oregano and seasoning. Mix in the tomato purée and cook for about five minutes. Pour the sauce over the pasta and add parmesan; stir well into the pasta and sprinkle with parmesan if desired.

PENNE WITH ARTICHOKE & TOMATO

This recipe reminds me of a weekend of walking and climbing in South Wales. The weather had that magical quality one sometimes gets in early autumn. The light was fantastic and a hint of mist lower down gave an atmospheric feel to the views from the Black Mountains. The day before had given us some immaculate rock climbing in the Gower Peninsula.

> **55g/2oz mushrooms, sliced**
> **1 small tin (225g/8oz) tomatoes**
> **1 onion, peeled and chopped**
> **1 clove garlic, peeled and chopped**
> **75ml/3fl oz red wine**
> **1 x 390g/13½oz tin artichoke hearts**

8 pitted olives, chopped
2 spoons olive oil
1 bay leaf
255g/9oz penne
45g/1½oz parmesan

Cook pasta as described on page 34.

Fry the onion and garlic in the oil until soft but not brown and then add the mushrooms and fry for a few minutes more. Add the tomatoes, wine and bay leaf and simmer for ten to 15 minutes, then remove the bay leaf. Drain and add the artichoke hearts — half a tin is probably enough, so take them in a resealable container and adjust the amount to taste. Add the olives and simmer for a further five minutes.

Pour over the pasta and sprinkle with parmesan. This seems to go particularly well with penne. If you can get fresh olives for this, the flavour is enhanced considerably.

Variation

The full recipe calls additionally for three anchovies and a spoonful of capers. If this is practical these should be added with the mushrooms and tomatoes respectively. Another variation if you cannot get hold of the artichokes, which can be elusive, is to substitute them with a couple of sticks of celery. In this case add the chopped celery with the tomatoes.

PEPPER & COURGETTE PASTA

This dish reminds me of a great summer walk up Ben Nevis (1344m/4409ft). It was summer by the calendar but the weather was otherwise, with a blizzard blowing on the top. The snow was wet and the footing very slippery so we had to move with great care as we took the classic traverse via the Carn Mor Dearg arête. Although an easy scramble in summer, this route can become an excellent winter outing with the right equipment and experience. On this occasion we were soon quite cold, not having expected the conditions, but this proved to be a good warming dish on the day.

    1 large onion, peeled and chopped
    1 clove garlic, peeled and chopped
    1 green pepper, seeded and diced
    1 red pepper, seeded and diced
    2 or 3 courgettes, sliced
    1 stick of celery or 1 large carrot, sliced
    100ml/4fl oz milk or cream
    1 tsp mixed herbs
    2 spoons olive oil or margarine
    255g/9oz pasta bows
    45g/1½oz parmesan (optional)

Cook pasta as described on page 34.

Fry the onion and garlic in the oil or margarine until soft but not brown. Add the peppers, courgettes, carrot or celery to the onion and continue to fry gently for five minutes, adding a little more oil if necessary to prevent burning. Pour in the milk or cream and add the herbs; cook for a further two minutes stirring continuously. Add salt and pepper to taste and a little water to dilute the sauce.

After serving with the pasta, sprinkle with parmesan if desired.

PESTO PASTA

Just about the easiest recipe you can have, but still one I really enjoy. A weekend of walking and climbing in Ardgour, to the west of Fort William, was the plan. However after walking from our campsite to the cliffs of Garbh Bheinn (885m/2903ft) we were greeted with some typical west coast weather. When we returned there was a problem crossing what had been a small stream on the inward journey! Nevertheless, given a break in the weather, this is an area not to be

missed. None of the hills here qualify as Munros,
all of them being below 3000ft.

255g/9oz pasta
1 small jar of pesto sauce

Cook pasta as described on page 34.
Drain the pasta and mix in the pesto sauce,
then serve.

Variation
Fry a little diced bacon, then add a small tub
of cream before stirring in the pesto sauce.

TUNA PASTA

This is probably my most standard of main
courses when camping and I have prepared this
many times in Scotland, against the backdrop of
a favourite Munro. One occasion that sticks in my
memory was at Shiel Bridge in Wester Ross,
where I had a beautiful view of the Five Sisters
of Kintail from the campsite. I had just
completed a long day traversing the South
Cluanie Ridge and this dish was the ideal end to
the day.

1 medium sized onion, peeled and
    chopped
1 clove garlic (optional), peeled and
    chopped
1 green pepper, seeded and chopped
1 x 200g/7oz tin tuna in brine (drained)
1 x 400g/14oz tin plum tomatoes
1 tsp dried herbs (tarragon or mixed)
2 spoons olive oil or margarine
255g/9oz pasta twists
30g/1oz parmesan (optional)

Cook pasta as described on page 34.
Fry the onion and garlic in the oil or margarine
until soft but not brown. Add the pepper to the

pan and fry for a couple of minutes more. Add tomatoes and drained tuna with dried tarragon or mixed herbs. Break up the tomatoes and tuna with a fork while stirring to mix ingredients thoroughly. Add pepper to taste (salt is rarely needed if the tuna was in brine) and continue to cook for a few minutes until really hot.

After serving with the pasta sprinkle with parmesan if desired.

Variation
A courgette or some cauliflower may be added or used as a substitute for the pepper.

WALNUT SAUCE

A simple but rich sauce, which does not need any cooking (though the pasta of course does), so this is a good option if you are wanting to conserve fuel. I used this the night before climbing the Dome de Neige des Ecrins, whilst bivvying near an overcrowded hut. The view was as sumptuous as the dish, and the peace I found away from the hut was idyllic.

10 shelled walnuts (i.e. 20 halves)
1 clove garlic, peeled and chopped
55g/2oz grated cheese
50ml/2fl oz olive oil
150ml/¼pt cream
1 spoon chopped parsley (optional)
255g/9oz pasta twirls

Cook pasta as described on page 34.

Crush the nuts as much as possible by hand or use a clean, large, rounded pebble as a pestle and a flatter one as a mortar; alternatively chop the nuts in a food processor at home and carry them ready-prepared. The cheese can be almost any type according to taste and availability; I tend to use a mixture of cheddar and parmesan. Reserve about a quarter of the cheese and mix all the remaining ingredients apart from the pasta, and whisk for a minute or two with a fork, seasoning to taste. Just before draining the pasta add a couple of spoons of the water in which it has cooked to the sauce. Optionally, warm the sauce gently, but ensure it does not boil. Mix the sauce with the drained pasta and sprinkle with the reserved grated cheese.

6

RICE DISHES

Rice is second only to pasta as a staple for backpacking. It is pretty indestructible and on a worldwide basis its availability is greater than any other food. Unlike pasta it requires boiling for the duration of its cooking time. Brown rice is healthier and tastier but requires twice as long to cook, so it's more convenient to use white rice for camping and backpacking. If you want to minimise cooking time, and fuel, check the packets on the supermarket shelves because different types vary in the cooking time required.

Rice can also be cooked in a pressure cooker, a valuable asset at altitude (see page 64 for a possible source). In this case cook with twice its volume of water; once the pressure has been reached continue to heat for one minute, then remove from heat and leave under pressure for seven minutes. Beans and lentils may also be pressure cooked, but to be safe with beans these should initially be boiled for ten minutes in the normal way. When cooking beans this way, the water will foam up and produce a lot of scum which needs to be skimmed off. If your pan is not that large this foam can tend to pour over the side, make a mess and extinguish the stove, so keep a close watch on the process.

Many of these dishes can also be served with other forms of carbohydrate. Being wheat derivatives, couscous and bulgur wheat are more related to pasta than rice, but both seem to provide a good accompaniment to dishes

normally associated with rice. These are
available from health food shops and have the
advantage of merely needing the addition of
approximately 2½ times their volume of boiling
water; no further cooking is required. After 15
minutes they are ready to eat, and during this
time you can prepare the main dish.

Unless rice is an integral part of the dish I
have not listed it as an ingredient. The easiest
way to cook rice is to add it to twice its volume of
boiling salted water, cover and simmer very
gently for about 12 minutes or until the rice is
cooked; the time will vary a bit with the variety.
A typical portion for two is about 200g/7oz.

CHILLI CON CARNE

Food has become very international and this is
now considered a 'traditional' dish. However it
was not in an international setting, but on a trip to
the spectacular scenery of the Assynt region in
North-west Scotland, where we first tried this out.
The higher peaks of Conival (987m/3238ft) and
Ben More Assynt (998m/3274ft) remain popular
but some of the smaller hills are unequalled.
Quinag (764m/2506ft) and Canisp (846m/2775ft)
are great Corbetts to climb, but capping them all is
the smaller Suilven (731m/2397ft), looking
impregnable from all aspects yet unfolding its
secrets on an interesting scramble.

> 350g/12oz minced beef
> 1 large onion, peeled and chopped
> 2 cloves garlic, peeled and chopped
> 1 x 400g/14oz tin tomatoes
> 1 x 400g/14oz tin pre-cooked kidney
>   beans, with or without chilli sauce
> 1 tsp chilli powder (if beans are without
>   sauce)
> 1 spoon flour
> 2 spoons olive oil or margarine

Fry the onion and garlic in the oil or margarine until soft but not brown. Add the mince and keep stirring well to prevent burning. Once the meat has begun to brown add the chilli powder and flour; continue to cook for a few minutes until the flour is absorbed. Add the tomatoes, pouring in the juice first while stirring well, and simmer gently for about 15 minutes. If the sauce becomes too thick, add a little water, or red wine. Add the beans and cook for another five to ten minutes. Serve with rice.

DALBHAT

Dalbhat is the staple food for many of the inhabitants of Nepal. We were in the remote Hinku valley on the approach to Mera Peak (6473m/21,246ft) when I first sampled it. After just two days walking from the airstrip at Lukla I reached this uninhabited valley. The many impressive peaks, most of which are probably rarely climbed, keep the days short and the shadows long, so keeping warm was a problem. Dalbhat was the fuel which kept us going.

200g/7oz red lentils
1 medium onion, peeled and chopped
1 tsp garam masala
½ tsp chilli powder (adjust quantity to taste)
2 spoons olive oil or margarine

Fry the onion in oil or margarine until soft but not brown; stir in the garam masala and chilli powder and cook a couple of minutes more. Add the lentils together with three times their volume of salted water. Bring to the boil and cook for about 20 minutes. The lentils used in Nepal take much longer to cook and our meals there were never quick, so I would not suggest being that authentic. Serve with rice or bulgur wheat.

Variation

This should ideally be accompanied by a spicy green vegetable. In this case leave out the chilli powder from the lentils; fry some chopped spring greens with the curry powder. After a few minutes add a little water; this will cook quite quickly.

FRIED RICE

The key difference between risotto (see page 60) and fried rice is that in the former the rice is fried before adding liquid whereas with fried rice, the frying is done after the rice is cooked. This was cooked in a hut in the Jotunheim region of Norway, but the dish is just as easy to prepare when camping. The Jotunheim is the most alpine of Norway's mountainous areas and includes the country's highest peaks, Galdhøppigen (2469m/8104ft) and Glittertind (2464m/8088ft). There is some debate about which is higher because it depends on whether the depth of snow counts as part of the mountain!

> **200g/7oz long grain rice**
> **1 medium onion, peeled and chopped**
> **2 eggs**
> **A few chopped vegetables (see text)**
> **2 spoons olive oil**
> **Soy sauce (optional)**

Cook the rice in plenty of boiling salted water for ten to 12 minutes, according to the variety (do not overcook); drain well. Fry the onion in the oil for a few minutes and then add a few spoonfuls of any chopped vegetables at hand such as carrots or peppers; alternatively add some dried peas or mixed vegetables to cook with the rice. After the carrots or peppers have softened, add the rice, stirring well. As soon as the rice and vegetables are well-mixed, add in the egg, continuing to stir;

season with pepper. Soy sauce can be added at this stage, if available.

Variation
A little cooked meat, such as chicken, can be added just before the rice.

LENTIL & MUSHROOM CASSEROLE

A solid winter-style dish to cast away the cold or wet. And wet it was when I visited the volcano of Tongariro (1976m/6485ft) in the centre of New Zealand's North Island. There are several volcanic hills in this region, and there is still quite a bit of activity associated with them. Plenty of good walking exists and, in winter, skiing. Indeed NZ's biggest ski area is on another volcano, Mt. Ruapehue (2797m/9180ft), where a short hike from the top of the ski-lifts produces stunning views into a steaming crater lake, recently the scene of rather too much volcanic activity.

140g/5oz red lentils
115g/4oz mushrooms, chopped fairly
   small
1 medium onion, peeled and chopped
55g/2oz cheddar cheese (grated or cut
   into small pieces)
4 spoons olive oil or margarine

Although green lentils probably make a slightly tastier dish, I tend to use red lentils when camping since they cook much more quickly. Boil the lentils in 2½ times their volume of salted water for 15-20 minutes until fairly soft, stirring occasionally to prevent them from burning. Either when cooked, (or part way through if you have a second stove), fry the onions in the oil or margarine until soft, but not brown. Add the mushrooms and cook well, seasoning with pepper. Stir in the lentils together with the cheese and mix well. This can be served on its own or with rice or bulgur wheat.

MUSHROOM CURRY

Friends of mine cooked this dish in a bothy on the Island of Hoy, Orkney, after a successful ascent of The Old Man of Hoy (137m/450ft). This spectacular tottering sea-stack became a TV 'personality' in the 1960's when the climb was brought live into people's living rooms by way of an outside broadcast which featured Tom Patey and Chris Bonington with Joe Brown, Ian McNaught-Davis, Dougal Haston and Peter Crew.

325g/11oz mushrooms
2 medium onions, peeled and chopped
1 clove garlic, peeled and chopped
2 sticks of celery (chopped)
1 green pepper, seeded and chopped
2 medium tomatoes, thickly sliced
**1 large cooking apple, peeled, cored and
    sliced**
4 spoons olive oil or margarine

The following can be combined at home in a poly bag (or take a ready-made curry powder mix):

½ tsp ground cumin
½ tsp ground cinnamon
½ tsp turmeric
½ tsp ground ginger
Pinch of cayenne pepper
¼ tsp ground cloves

Fry the onion and garlic in the oil or margarine for a couple of minutes and then add the spices. When the onion has softened add the pepper, mushrooms, celery and about half-a-cup of water to prevent sticking. Simmer for five to eight minutes, when the celery is slightly tender then add the apple and tomato. Remove from the heat, add a little more water if too dry (or lemon juice if you have it); mix and let it stand for a few minutes. Serve with rice.

NUTTY RICE PILAFF

A favourite recipe from friends who used this while camping at a picturesque isolated lake in the John Muir Wilderness, the High Sierras of California. The variant was born of necessity in Chile where apricots were not available. There is plenty of superb trekking and the Torres del Paines (approx 2900m/9500ft) rise spectacularly from the Patagonian pampas. When cold, this dish also makes a good lunch.

140g/5oz rice
1 stock cube, vegetable or chicken
55g/2oz raisins
55g/2oz chopped dried apricots
55g/2oz pistachios or peanuts

Soak the raisins in water for about 20 minutes. Cook the rice gently in twice its volume of salted water, together with the crumbled stock cube, until nearly done. This will take around ten minutes for white rice or 20 minutes for the tastier brown rice. Put the apricots, raisins and nuts on top and leave, covered, for a couple of minutes on a gentle heat. Stir everything together and serve.

Variation
Leave out the apricots, but add about half a fresh chilli to the rice at the start of cooking; a few mushrooms can also be added part-way through the cooking.

POTATO & CAULIFLOWER CURRY

This is a simple curry, but it is quite filling. As the ingredients are a bit heavy I use it when car-camping and first tried it on a night below Creag Meagaidh (1130m/3707ft) near Spean Bridge. The following morning was very grey and misty and we were not expecting to see much. Just a few feet below the summit we broke through the mist to a fantastic view of the peaks poking up through a sea of cloud. To add to the overall effect we were also rewarded with a 'glory' when our shadows were projected onto the clouds and surrounded by rainbows.

450g/1lb potatoes
Half a medium cauliflower, cut into fairly
    small pieces.
1 large onion, peeled and chopped
1-2 tsp curry powder (according to taste)
1 vegetable stock cube
4 spoons olive oil or margarine

Boil the potatoes for ten minutes and then add the cauliflower. Do not allow either to become too soft, probably about 15 minutes in total (i.e. five minutes for the cauliflower) will do. Drain and slice or chop the potatoes into thick pieces. Fry the onion in the oil or margarine for a couple of minutes before adding the curry powder. (If you like your curries hot you may also want to add some dried chillies.) After a couple of minutes add the potato and cauliflower and a pinch of salt, mixing well. Either sprinkle in a crumbled stock cube and add about 300ml/½pt of water, or make up the stock first and then add it. Cook for a few minutes more, adding a little more water if it is too dry. Serve with rice.

RICE WITH CABBAGE

This was a welcome meal after a damp day of walking during a Norwegian autumn. Although not far from the populated areas around Stavanger, we were soon in wild country. Apart from the hills I recall particularly the many lemmings which scurried around as we walked along. We climbed a peak called Snønuten (1606m/5269ft), which is the highest point in the area, and it was a great introduction to the country, even if the weather was less than perfect. It turned out to be a long day, with the last three hours spent walking in the dark before reaching our objective for the night.

400g/14oz savoy or white cabbage
200g/7oz rice
2 or 3 rashers streaky bacon (optional), chopped
1 large onion, peeled and chopped
1 stock cube, vegetable or beef
2 spoons olive oil or margarine
55g/2oz grated cheese

Slice the cabbage thinly; I prefer savoy to white cabbage but this is not always as easy to obtain. Fry the onion and the bacon (which may be omitted if you want a vegetarian dish), in the oil or margarine for a few minutes. Then add the cabbage, season with pepper and stir well, continuing to fry for a further three to four minutes. Dissolve the stock cube in twice the volume of boiling water to rice, then add this with the rice to the cabbage. Bring to the boil and simmer for ten to 12 minutes, adding a little more water if necessary towards the end of cooking. Add in the cheese, mix well and serve.

Variation
Increase the quantity of water to make this into a thick soup.

RICE WITH TOMATO & BASIL

Quick and simple, and if you can get fresh ingredients, as I did in southern France, the flavour is superb. I was near the small village of La Grave, between Grenoble and Briançon, when I first made this. This village has become better known in the last few years for its off-piste skiing, but is still fortunately a far cry from most overcrowded French ski resorts. It is a beautiful spot in summer, with the imposing peak of La Meije (3983m/13,068ft) providing a magnificent backdrop.

255g/9oz rice
4 medium size ripe tomatoes
2 cloves garlic, peeled and chopped
Several leaves fresh basil, chopped
6 spoons olive oil
4 spoons tomato purée (see text)
30-55g/1-2oz grated cheese (optional)

Cover the rice in twice its volume of boiling salted water and continue to simmer until just cooked (about 12 minutes). Fry the garlic in the oil for a couple of minutes and then add the tomatoes and basil. The former should be plum tomatoes, but if not add tomato purée after the tomatoes have softened to enhance the flavour. Season well and add a little water to make the mixture into a fairly thick sauce. Drain the rice and mix well with the sauce. If desired, top it all with some grated cheese.

RISOTTO

Although risotto should use a shorter grain Italian rice, I tend to use long grain rice because it is a standard item from the kitchen shelf. Memories here are evoked of sunshine and lazing about on beaches while spending a New Year on the Abel Tasman Track, which lies at the north end of New Zealand's South Island. The scenery is uniquely Kiwi, with lush rain forest adjoining golden beaches which regrettably are becoming more overcrowded. You can always do some sea-kayaking to avoid the crush!

200g/7oz rice
1 medium onion, peeled and chopped
75ml/3fl oz dry white wine (optional)
1 stock cube, vegetable or beef
1 spoon olive oil
1 spoon margarine
30g/1oz parmesan, grated

Fry the onion in the oil until soft but not brown. Add the rice and stir well for about a minute. Add the wine if used, and then gradually about ½litre/¾pint water together with the crumbled stock cube. Bring to the boil and let it cook gently until the rice is just cooked, about 12 minutes. Remove from the heat and stir in the margarine, grated parmesan and pepper to taste; mix well.

Variation
A few chopped vegetables can be added at the start for a bit of variety.

VEGETARIAN CHILLI

I cooked this one for a group of climbing friends at the Spanish village of El Chorro, just north of Malaga. This is a good place for a week of 'sun-rock' as there is plenty of excellent rock, much of it forming a very dramatic gorge. There is an amazing construction running along this gorge, The King's Way, which juts out from the sheer cliffs with a huge drop below. Now that much of the guard-rail has disappeared, it is certainly only for those with a good head for heights.

1 x 400g/14oz tin pre-cooked kidney
    beans
1 x 400g/14oz tin tomatoes
1 medium onion, peeled and chopped
2 cloves garlic, peeled and crushed
1 carrot, chopped
Half a green pepper, seeded and chopped
A few green beans, or 1 courgette,
    chopped
50ml/2fl oz red wine (optional)
2 spoons olive oil
½ tsp (adjust to taste) chilli powder

Fry the onion and garlic in the oil until soft
but not brown. Add in the chopped carrot, salt
pepper and spices and cook for about ten
minutes until just tender; add the pepper and
green beans/courgette; cook for a couple more
minutes. Add the red wine, tinned tomatoes and
beans and heat through. Serve with rice or bulgur
wheat.

Variation
You can also vary the vegetables according to
what is available.

7

OTHER MAIN COURSES

I have included quite a variety of dishes here, some vegetarian (though the pasta and rice sections have a higher proportion of vegetarian food), some fish and some meat-based. Many of these are adapted from home recipes and simplified to be more practical for cooking on a camp stove.

Casseroles and stews can be very appetising and nourishing, but unfortunately do require a lot of cooking. There are three solutions to this in the camping environment. The first is to cook the dish at home (see also chapter 10) and just heat it up at your campsite, making sure the container you use is well-sealed.

Solution number two is the 'haybox' system. Carry out the initial cooking of the dish by frying the ingredients, adding liquid, bringing to the boil for about five minutes and then wrapping the pan in a cloth or old T-shirt and placing the whole thing in a sleeping bag (the cloth is just to stop any soot etc. getting on the sleeping bag). Leave for four hours or more while you go off for your day's walking. When you want to eat all you need to do is reheat; you may wish to simmer for up to 20 minutes if you want to cook it a little more.

The final method is to use a pressure cooker. Pressure cookers also come into their own for cooking basics, such as rice, at high altitude. A small pressure cooker costing around £50 and designed for two-man expedition use is available from Doug Scott, Chapel House, Low Cotehill,

Carlisle, CA4 0EL. Though not cheap, the saving in fuel plus the added benefit of better food in a mountain environment make it a useful addition, especially for an expedition to higher altitudes.

BEEF STROGANOFF

Another classic dish, though one which seems to have gone out of the limelight a little. It lends itself well to the camping environment especially if you miss out the sour cream and use dried milk instead. Admittedly it's not quite as authentic as the original recipe, but it still tastes pretty good, especially after a day such as the one I had on Ben Cruachan (1126m/3694ft) in Argyll. Although clear it was windy and none too warm as I made a circuit including the two Munros just to the north, Beinn a'Chocuill (980m/3215ft) and Beinn Eunaich (989m/3245ft). The views from Cruachan south along Loch Awe are spectacular, particularly at sunset.

> 325g/11oz topside of beef (or chuck steak)
> 115g/4oz mushrooms (sliced if large; if small, add them whole)
> 1 clove garlic, peeled and chopped
> 1 small onion, peeled and chopped
> Half a beef stock cube
> 2 spoons tomato purée
> 2 spoons olive oil or margarine
> 2 spoons flour, seasoned with salt and pepper for coating the meat
> 75ml/3fl oz sour cream, or equivalent dried milk plus 1 tsp paprika

Dissolve the half stock cube in 150ml/¼pt hot water in a mug.

Cut the beef into thin strips and coat in the seasoned flour. Heat half the oil or margarine until very hot and add the beef strips, stirring to

prevent them sticking, for one to two minutes.
Remove the beef and put to one side. Add the
remaining oil/margarine and reduce the heat; add
the garlic and onion and fry for about three
minutes before adding the mushrooms and fry
for a further two minutes. Add the stock and
tomato purée and cook for a couple of minutes,
stirring well. Add the beef to the sauce and heat
through.

Remove the pan from the heat and stir in the
sour cream. If using milk and paprika, add this
with the beef.

Serve with boiled rice, or noodles.

CHEESE FONDUE

A fondue is a simple and very sociable way of
eating. You need a stove which can be properly
regulated and a pan (non-stick preferably). Such
a recipe must naturally conjure up images of
Switzerland. We had just completed an ascent of
a classic rock climb, the Miroir d'Argentine, near
the ski-resort of Villars, a very enjoyable route of
some 14 pitches (rope lengths), or about
600m/1970ft with the bonus of a pleasant scenic
descent through alpine meadows — real
chocolate box stuff!

**85g/3oz feta cheese, grated or in small
    pieces
170g/6oz ricotta cheese, grated or in
    small pieces
100ml/4fl oz dry white wine
1 clove garlic, crushed
1 spoon olive oil or margarine
¼ tsp grated nutmeg (optional)
30ml/1fl oz kirsch (optional)
1 French stick or similar amount of other
    bread**

Fry the garlic for a minute in the oil or
margarine. Add the wine and heat gently. Stir in

the cheese and keep stirring until it has melted to form a fairly thick sauce. Add a little more wine if it is too thick. Stir in the nutmeg, kirsch and a little black pepper. Reduce heat until the cheese is just bubbling gently.

The fondue is now ready to serve. Chop or break the bread into small pieces and using a normal fork, or better still, proper fondue forks, dip the bread into the fondue and gather as much of the cheese sauce as your friends will let you!

Variation

Alternative cheeses such as emmental or gruyère can also be used; I'm sure connoisseurs of fondues will have their own views on their favourite cheeses to use.

CHICKEN LIVERS WITH EGGS

I've suggested serving this with fresh bread. Combined with the fact that chicken livers are not always the easiest item to come by in Britain, this is another dish with a French bias. I tasted this in the beautiful village of Orpierre, a 1½ hour drive north of Marseilles. This is a rock climber's paradise with extensive climbing at all points of the compass. The campsite in the village gives special rates to climbers, so make sure you take advantage of this.

255g/9oz chicken livers
1 small onion, peeled and chopped
1 medium tomato, chopped
1 red pepper, chopped
(or use 1x 200g/7oz tin of tomatoes
    instead of the tomato and pepper)
2 eggs
2 spoons olive oil
1 tsp mixed herbs

Fry the chicken livers in half the oil until browned on the outside and put them to one side. Fry the onion and the red pepper (if used), until soft but not brown. Add the tomatoes and herbs and cook for five minutes before returning the liver to the pan for a minute. Break the eggs into the pan, ideally without breaking the yolks. Cover and cook gently until they are just set.

This goes well served with a fresh green vegetable such as french beans, along with rice or some crusty fresh bread, if available.

Variation
Use lamb's or pig's liver, sliced thinly, if chicken livers are not available.

CHICKEN WITH APPLE SAUCE

An unusual combination of flavours and an easy dish to cook. Pre-cook the chicken at home, or just take the leftovers from a roast chicken. For me, this evokes a taste of North Wales where I was camped beneath the wonderful cliffs of Cwm Idwal. What better place to experience the accessible magic of wild Snowdonia?

225g/8oz cooked chicken
1 apple, peeled, cored and chopped
1 small onion, peeled and chopped
1 stick celery, chopped
55g/2oz margarine
75ml/3fl oz double cream
1 spoon flour

Fry the celery and onion in half the margarine for a couple of minutes and then add the apple and cook for a couple of minutes more. Add 75ml/3fl oz of water, a little salt and pepper and simmer for a further two minutes until reduced by at least half and set this to one side. In another pan melt the remaining margarine, stir in the flour and cook for a minute before gradually adding the cream or milk. Cook gently until the sauce thickens. Add the chicken to the sauce and then add the apple/vegetable mixture. Keep on the stove over a gentle heat until hot right through. This is best served with instant mashed potatoes or noodles.

Variation
The celery may be omitted if not readily available. Try using a carrot in its place.

CHICKEN WITH WILD MUSHROOMS

This is a superb dish if you can lay you hands on the chanterelles. I have to thank Nick Nairn of the Braeval Old Mill Restaurant at Aberfoyle for my introduction to these and for this recipe. We found the chanterelles in the vicinity of the Crianlarich Hills at the head of Loch Lomond, but I'm not giving away any more! This group of hills holds more interest than may at first appear where the shapely ridges linking Beinn Chabhair (933m/3061ft), Beinn a'Chroin (940m/3084ft) and An Caisteal (995m/3264ft) form a great day's walking. The descent along Twistin' Hill crosses an interesting and unusual cleft, only a foot or so wide but very deep.

> 255g/9oz chicken breast (boneless)
> 1 small onion, peeled and chopped
> 1 clove garlic, peeled and chopped
> 1 cupful chanterelles or other wild
>   mushrooms
> 100ml/4fl oz dry white wine
> 100ml/4fl oz cream
> 3 spoons olive oil
> 2 spoons margarine
> 1 tsp dried, or 1 spoon fresh, mixed
>   herbs or tarragon

Fry the onion and garlic in one spoonful of oil until soft but not brown. Slice the chicken into thin strips. Increase the heat and ensure the oil is hot before adding the chicken strips and stir well for a few minutes until cooked through. Remove the chicken and as much onion as possible from the pan and set this to one side. Clean the chanterelles and slice the larger ones. Add a spoonful each of oil and margarine to the pan and when hot add the mushrooms and fry until liquid comes out of them. This is mostly water so drain the chanterelles and put them to one side. Add the remaining oil and margarine to the pan and return to the heat. Once this is hot, return the chanterelles to the pan and fry for a minute before adding the chicken, onion, white wine and herbs. Cook gently until the wine has reduced by half and then stir in the cream and cook for a further minute. Season to taste.

Serve with rice or boiled potatoes and a simple green vegetable such as peas.

Variation

If chanterelles are not available use other wild, or cultivated mushrooms. In this case omit the first stage of cooking the mushrooms and reduce the quantity of oil and margarine by half.

CORNED BEEF HASH

An old-fashioned recipe that still provides a tasty and nourishing meal, even if it doesn't always look the most appetising! I was in the final throes of my Munro-bagging, ticking off the lone peak of Ben Bhuidhe in Argyll (948m/3110ft). Whilst not a particularly special peak in itself, its isolation allows it to command magnificent views over the islands of Mull, Jura and Arran, especially at sunset.

1 x 350g/12oz tin corned beef
1 medium onion, peeled and chopped
Half a red or green pepper, seeded and
   chopped
115g/4oz mushrooms
Small packet freeze-dried vegetables (see
   text)

2 spoons olive oil or margarine
1 packet instant mash, or 450g/1lb
   potatoes

Boil the potatoes and mash them, using the water they cooked in to reconstitute the dried vegetables. I prefer peas as the freeze-dried vegetable but these seem to be rarely available so mixed-vegetables might be used instead. Fry the onion in the oil or margarine until soft but not brown, then add the pepper and sliced mushrooms. Flake in the corned beef and stir until heated through. Serve with the mashed potato or mix it all together if you prefer.

EGGS AFRICAN

A recipe from Kenya, this can either form a substantial breakfast dish or the basis of a main meal, served with fried potatoes or pitta bread. When eating this I imagine the wonderful snow-capped cone of Kilimanjaro (5895m/19,341ft) in the background, with some of the magnificent African wildlife grazing on the plains below.

4 eggs
1 medium onion, peeled and thinly sliced
1 red pepper, seeded and chopped
115g/4oz mushrooms, sliced
30g/1oz margarine
¼ tsp chilli powder (optional)

Gently fry the onion and pepper until soft and then add the mushrooms. When the mushrooms have softened add the chilli powder, if desired, and cook for another minute. Beat the eggs with a little salt and pepper and add these to the pan, stirring constantly. If the pan looks a bit dry after cooking the mushrooms, add a little more oil or margarine.

FISH CAKES

This is a simple dish and one which can be very convenient if you catch your own fish. I've been warmed up by eating this on a cool day with cloudy skies along the shores of Loch Bhrotain, which sits beneath the Fannichs near Garve in Sutherland. These are a great range of hills, with a really remote feeling to them, yet they are not really that far away from the road. It is probably the lack of any habitation along that part of the road which enhances the feeling of isolation and peace.

> **325g/11oz white fish (cod, haddock etc.)**
> **450g/1lb potatoes, or 1 packet instant mashed potato**
> **1 spoon chopped fresh parsley or 1 tsp dried mixed herbs**
> **1 small onion, peeled and chopped (optional)**
> **1 egg**
> **3-4 spoons margarine**

Boil the potatoes and when these are ready, cook the fish as follows. In the frying pan, poach the fish gently for two to five minutes (depending on thickness), in as little water as possible, until just cooked. While the fish is cooking, mash the potatoes, adding a little margarine to soften this.

Drain the fish and flake it into the potato. Add the onion (if using), egg, chopped parsley, (or dried mixed herbs if parsley is not available), and pepper to taste. Mix well and then form into about four fish cakes. Heat two spoons of margarine and once hot, add the fish cakes and cook each side for two to three minutes. Serve with a green vegetable or mixed salad.

If using instant mashed potato, use the water in which the fish was poached as part of the water for reconstituting the potato.

Variation
Coat the fishcakes in breadcrumbs before frying to give a more finished appearance. The egg is not essential, but does help to bind the fishcakes together.

FISH IN CHEESE SAUCE

This was my first attempt at cooking a dish based on white sauce on a camping stove, but it proved quite straightforward. Near Avignon lie the Dentelles de Montmirail which comprise scattered outcrops of limestone, providing not only climbing but even better general walking. It is all quite low level, so a good option for poor weather.

> **285g/10oz white fish**
> **55g/2oz cheddar cheese (or another variety, such as emmental), grated**
> **300ml/½pt milk**
> **30g/1oz flour (2 rounded spoonfuls)**
> **30g/1oz margarine**
> **A few herbs if available**

Cover the fish in water and add about four spoons of milk. If herbs are to hand add about a spoonful; tarragon and/or a bayleaf are ideal. Bring gently to the boil and simmer for five minutes and then remove from the heat, but leave the fish in the liquid since it will continue to cook while you prepare the sauce. Melt the margarine and stir in the flour, cooking for a minute before gradually adding the milk, stirring to prevent lumps and cook until a white sauce has been created. Season and gradually add the cheese; continue to stir until the cheese has all melted. Check that fish is cooked and if necessary return to the heat for a few minutes more; drain the fish and serve, pouring the cheese sauce over it.

FISH STEW

Another way to cook fish you have just caught! I've only done this with bought fish, but tinned can also be used (see variation). Local ingredients were used the first time I made this. Montserrat, a short drive from Barcelona, not only boasts a famous monastery but also plenty of excellent bolted rock climbing on numerous conglomerate towers and outcrops. These form a compact range of hills jutting up dramatically from the plains below.

325g/11oz white fish, cut into pieces
1 onion, peeled and chopped
1 carrot, chopped
1 medium potato, peeled and chopped
300ml/½pt fish, chicken or vegetable
    stock
50ml/2fl oz dry white wine
2 spoons olive oil
1 bayleaf
50ml/2fl oz double cream (optional)

Fry the onion, potato and carrot in the oil for ten minutes. Add the stock, wine, bayleaf and seasoning; bring to the boil and simmer for ten minutes. Add the fish and simmer for a further three minutes. Stir in the double cream (optional) and serve with mashed potatoes.

Variation
Instead of serving with mash, use a large pan and increase the quantity of potato to 450g/1lb; everything for the meal is then cooked together.

This can also be used with a tin of fish, such as tuna.

FRIED TROUT

While spending some time in New Zealand I had missed eating trout since it cannot be sold over there; you have either to catch it or be given it. After a hard day cycling up a rough road over Danzey's Pass in the South Island, I had hoped to camp at the village of Duntroon, but on reaching it found neither campsite nor shop. I carried on along the Waitaki Valley towards Lake Aviemore. There, I was given a beautiful trout by the kind campsite owner and cycled a few kilometres back down the road to a fruit and vegetable stall for some suitable accompaniments.

**2 small trout
2 spoons margarine
A few flaked almonds (optional)
Juice of half a lemon**

Small trout are easier to fit in a camping pan, but you may have to chop up your fish. This doesn't spoil the taste, but a whole fish does look a lot more impressive. Gut and wash the trout. Fry for about five minutes on each side or until the fish is cooked through and the flesh is firm, adding the almonds halfway through. Sprinkle with a little lemon juice and serve with potatoes and fresh vegetables. Trout can of course also be barbecued, either directly on a griddle, or baked in foil on a campfire (allow about 15-20 minutes). In the latter case you can easily have jacket potatoes on the side.

KEDGEREE

Kedgeree was a breakfast dish in Victorian times, but most would now consider it a bit more of a main course, although if you need fortifying for a Scottish winter day's walking you could start the day this way. It was a winter day for me, but this was dinner after a walk over Ben Lui (1130m/3707ft) and Ben Oss (1028m/3373ft) near Tyndrum. This predates my climbing days so I have yet to return to ascend the attractive Central Gully of the former peak.

255g/9oz smoked haddock
200g/7oz rice
1 egg
2 spoons margarine
½ to 1 tsp curry powder (optional)

Hard-boil the egg in advance. Cover the haddock in water, or a mixture of water and milk and bring gently to the boil. Remove from the heat, cover and put to one side; the fish will cook in this way while the rice is prepared. Cook the rice in plenty of boiling salted water for about 12 minutes, depending on the variety. Drain the rice and flake the fish into it. Melt the margarine in the now empty fish pan, add the rice, fish and chop the egg into this. Stir occasionally, adding the curry powder if desired and continue to cook until heated right through. If you do decide to try this for breakfast, the fish and rice can be cooked the night before; it will just take a few extra minutes to heat the dish the next morning.

KIDNEY BEAN & LENTIL CASSEROLE

As both the main ingredients need soaking this is an ideal dish when you are camped at the same place for a couple of nights. The beans and lentils can be left to soak while you're out walking during the day. Alternatively you can employ red lentils and tinned beans. This dish does also need a bit more cooking time than some; if you have a camp fire going it can simmer on that for the best part of it. I tried this when I was staying at a bothy this time, Culra, which sits below Ben Alder (1148m/3766ft) near Loch Ericht with a good number of Munros within easy reach. This whole area is one of the largest tracts of wilderness in Scotland not dissected by any public road and gives ideal walking terrain for a two-day expedition. In winter it feels very remote but as long as you are suitably equipped and experienced, it is a superb place to explore.

1 onion, peeled and chopped
1 clove garlic, peeled and chopped
Half a red pepper, chopped
1 x 400g/14oz tin tomatoes
115g/4oz red kidney beans
85g/3oz whole green lentils
½ tsp paprika
¼ to ½ tsp chilli powder
2 spoons olive oil or margarine
1 spoon sugar

Leave the kidney beans and lentils to soak (separately) for several hours. Cook the beans for about 40 minutes and the lentils for 20 minutes, ensuring the beans are boiled rapidly for ten minutes, then simmered for the remainder of the cooking time; if you only have one stove this can be done one after the other.

Fry the onions, garlic and pepper in the oil or margarine for ten minutes and then add the tomatoes and cook for a further couple of minutes. Drain the beans and lentils and add to the tomato mixture. Add the paprika and chilli powder and simmer for 15 minutes. Season to taste.

Variation
If using tinned beans, add these with the tomatoes.

KIPPER SCRAMBLE

This can either be a main course if served with some sturdy carbohydrate — perhaps fried potatoes — or a somewhat different start to the day. It was as a hearty breakfast in the Torridon area that I first tried this. A walk up Ben Alligin (985m/3232ft) and a scramble around the Horns of Alligin made an interesting winter day's outing. Not only is this a great hill in its own right but the views across to its bigger brothers, such as Liathach (1054m/3458ft), give the summit outlook an extra, almost Alpine, dimension.

170g/6oz kipper fillets
2 eggs
1 spoon margarine
3 spoons single cream (optional)

Melt the margarine and flake the kippers into this, avoiding adding the skin. Cook for a couple of minutes and then add the eggs and a little pepper. Stir continuously until lightly cooked. Add the cream just before serving, if desired.

LIVER & ONIONS

I'm very fond of liver but I know it's not to everyone's taste. However I recommend you to be adventurous and try this delicious dish. Needless to say if you are backpacking you need to be very careful about carrying liver, since it can get very messy! The Isle of Mull is recalled; a beautiful crossing from Oban on the early morning ferry, but by the time I reached the summit of Ben More (966m/3169ft) the visibility was down to 50 metres, so the views were restricted. Mull has much to offer with great coastal scenery as well as hills.

255g/9oz calves liver
1 large onion, peeled and sliced
1 clove garlic, peeled and chopped
1 spoon flour
1 beef stock cube, made up into
    300ml/½pt stock
2 spoons olive oil or margarine

Fry the onion and garlic in the oil or margarine for a couple of minutes. Cut the liver into thin strips and coat with the flour and add this to the pan. Fry for about three minutes, turning occasionally to ensure the meat is browned. Add a little more oil if it seems too dry. Add the stock gradually and stir well; simmer for about ten minutes, seasoning to taste.

Serve with potatoes, rice, or noodles.

LIVER IN WINE

As mentioned in the recipe for liver and onions you need to be very careful when carrying liver to ensure there are no leaks. A visit to the Pyrenees was the setting for this delicious way of preparing liver. The small village of Lescun nestles amongst some dramatic peaks forming a 'cirque' of the same name. A walk through lush vegetation brought me to a selection of peaks, several with good rock-climbing potential. On reaching the summit ridge, the arid appearance on the Spanish side of the range provided a striking contrast.

225g/9oz calves liver
1 clove garlic, peeled and chopped
100ml/4fl oz dry white wine
100ml/4fl oz sour cream
2 spoons flour
3 spoons olive oil or margarine
2 spoons fresh parsley or 1 tsp dried
      herbs

Fry the garlic in the oil or margarine for a couple of minutes. Cut the liver into thin strips and coat with the flour and add this to the pan. Fry for about three minutes, turning occasionally to ensure the meat is browned. Remove and put to one side.

Pour the wine into the pan with the parsley or other herbs. Stir well and simmer until reduced by half. Add the sour cream, season and return the liver to the pan to heat through.

Serve with potatoes, rice, or noodles.

MOULES MARINIÈRE

If you're able to collect the mussels yourself while walking along a rocky seashore this is an ideal meal. I was spending a few days mountain-biking around Great Barrier Island which lies a short boat trip east of the North Island of New Zealand. A hilly and well-forested area, it has great biking and walking potential with some beautiful beaches and camping spots.

> **About 1½litres/2½pt mussels**
> **1 small onion, peeled and chopped**
> **150ml/¼pt dry white wine**
> **1 spoon margarine**
> **1 tsp dried mixed herbs or 1 spoon fresh parsley**

The chances are you will need to cook this in two batches as it requires a fairly large pan. Clean the mussels in a pan of cold water by de-bearding them and ensuring that loose material and barnacles are scraped from the shells. If any of them remain open after this, discard them immediately. Put all the ingredients into a large pan and cover. Cook for a few minutes over a moderate heat, stirring or shaking occasionally. When all the mussels have opened they are ready to eat; discard any which have not opened.

NUTTY LAMB MEATBALLS

Where better for a lamb recipe than New Zealand? I had a truly superb winter's day one August, making an ascent of Mount Rolleston (2272m/7454ft) via a classic route, the Otira Face. This peak is one of the most accessible in the country, being only a two-hour drive from Christchurch and lacking a long walk-in. The snow was in excellent condition with perfect névé making the going straightforward. As we came out of the shadow of the adjacent tops we were soon baking in the hot sun. Once on the summit ridge we were rewarded with views right across to the West coast, displaying just how many mountains there are in the region.

325g/11oz minced lamb
Half a small red pepper, seeded and finely
    chopped
30g/1oz shelled almonds or walnuts,
    crushed or chopped finely
1 clove garlic, peeled and chopped
½ tsp ground ginger
3 spoons orange juice
3 spoons apricot jam
3 spoons olive oil
1 egg (optional)

Mix the nuts with the lamb, pepper, garlic, nuts, ginger and seasoning. Add an egg (if using) since it helps to bind the mixture, but this can be omitted. Press firmly into four or six meatballs or burgers. Mix the orange juice, apricot jam and oil together and heat in a pan, stirring all the time. Once this is hot add the meatballs and fry for about eight minutes, turning occasionally. Serve with rice or mashed potatoes.

OMELETTES

Carrying eggs is not always the easiest thing to do. You can, however, buy plastic egg containers at some outdoor shops. On longer walks you might be passing through a village or past a farm where they are available; eggs can be bought in just about any part of the world and are a welcome break to a more mundane diet based on dried ingredients. This reminds me of some great walking in rural France, along parts of the Jura mountains near the Swiss border.

6 eggs
2-4 spoons margarine or butter
Any of the following makes a good filling:

115g/4oz mushrooms
2 tomatoes
A couple of slices of ham, chopped.
Just a few herbs (fresh if possible)

First prepare the filling. Slice the mushrooms or tomatoes and fry in one or two spoons of margarine or butter until just cooked, but not too soft and put this to one side. Add the ham. For consistency with the other recipes the quantities here are for two, but you'll need to cook the omelettes individually. Whisk three eggs slightly with just a splash of water plus seasoning; if the filling is going to be herbs, these should be added at this stage. Heat a spoonful of margarine, or butter if possible, until good and hot, preferably in a non-stick frying pan, and add the egg mixture.

With a spoon gently draw the mixture in from the sides of the pan as it cooks, allowing the uncooked egg to leak out to the edges to cook. Continue this until the top of the eggs is still runny and then turn half the filling over the other half; serve. The inside will continue to cook a little after removed from the pan. Repeat for the other omelette.

RED PEPPER (SPANISH) OMELETTE

This can be prepared with either red or green pepper but I prefer the sweeter red ones which seem to give more of the sunny feeling of Spain; you may have had this in a tapas bar somewhere! We were on a climbing trip to Mallorca one New Year when I came across this in a bar in the village of Calvia. The climbing around here is good, but the walking probably even better.

4 eggs, or equivalent amount of dried egg
1 onion, peeled and sliced
1 red pepper, thinly sliced
1-2 potatoes, thinly sliced
2 spoons olive oil or margarine

Beat the eggs well with a little salt and pepper, or reconstitute the dried egg with water. Fry the vegetables in half the oil or margarine until tender but not mushy; drain well and stir into the eggs. Heat the remaining oil/margarine until sizzling; add the mixture and reduce the heat, cooking until the omelette is firm underneath. Turn it over with a fish slice (or turn it out on to a plate to make this job easier), adding a little more oil if necessary. Cook until firm but still slightly moist inside.

Variation

You can also use cold potatoes or other vegetables, so this can be a great way to use leftovers.

QUICK COWBOY TEA

With this name, it has to be in a western United States location when I first tasted this. Canyonlands National Park in Utah is an eerie place at night, with huge sandstone formations everywhere. Utah has plenty of desert areas such as this and it is easy to imagine being transported back a hundred years. Not much changes in the desert, and it can be chilly at night; this is a warming meal, on such occasions.

> 1 large onion, peeled and chopped
> 450g/1lb sausages
> 1 x 425g/15oz tin baked beans
> 1 spoon olive oil or margarine
> ½-1 tsp chilli powder (optional)
> 1 x 400g/14oz tin pre-cooked, red kidney
>   beans (optional)

Fry the onion in the oil or margarine until soft but not brown; add chilli powder (if used) and fry for a couple of minutes more. Add the sausages and fry until brown and cooked through. Add the tin of beans and heat through.

Serve with chunks of bread or pitta bread.

SALMON IN WHITE WINE

Another one which originated from the United States. I was in the region of the glitzy ski resort of Aspen in the summer when it is a walker's paradise. Despite the crowds in the town and on the roads, an hour's hike to a small lake gave me a tranquil camping spot nestling near the imposing local mountains, the Maroon Bells, which reminded me of Liathach in Torridon.

2 salmon steaks, each about 170g/6oz
2 spoons margarine or butter
100ml/4fl oz dry white wine
1 tsp tarragon

Fry the salmon steaks gently for a couple of minutes on each side in the margarine or butter and then add wine, tarragon and season to taste. Cook gently for about five minutes, turning the fish once. Serve with mashed potatoes and peas or green beans.

SAVOURY PANCAKES

Pancakes are not as difficult to make as it may first seem, especially if ready-made pancake mix is used; I've also given the full recipe for pancakes as a dessert (see page 95). A non-stick pan is recommended; another good way to cook them is on a griddle if you are having a barbecue. These pancakes were sampled on 90-mile Beach in the very north of New Zealand where you can drive for many miles along the beach when the tide is out. There are huge sand dunes just inland and great fun can be had sliding down these on body boards (really designed for riding the waves!) If you know where to look you can also collect seafood to use as a filling for the pancakes.

**1 x 90g packet pancake mix, or use part
of a larger packet
140g/5oz white fish or fresh seafood
Half a red pepper, seeded and chopped
A few mushrooms, sliced or chopped
2 spoons olive oil or margarine**

Make up the pancake mixture according to
the manufacturer's instructions. Chop the fish
into small pieces and fry with the pepper and
mushrooms in half the oil or margarine, turning
the fish from time to time. When just cooked
through, which will take about five minutes, put
this to one side while cooking pancakes.

Heat a little oil/margarine and pour in just
enough mixture to cover the pan; cook until
bubbles appear and then turn to cook the other
side. Put in some of the fish and vegetable
mixture, roll up and serve. If you are feeling
ambitious and have a second stove you can make
a white sauce (see recipe for Fish in Cheese
Sauce on page 72 but omit the cheese).

Variation

As an alternative to filling the pancakes, add
some fried chopped vegetables to the pancake
mixture and make the pancakes a bit thicker.

SOYA MINCE COTTAGE PIE

Introduced to me one wet weekend in the
North-west Highlands of Scotland, I recall
cooking this at lunchtime next to the car after we
had retreated from two nearby Munros. We
received some flack from our friends who were
more dedicated to peak-bagging in miserable
conditions! The Munros were just to the north of
Loch Quoich overlooking Glen Sheil and when I
returned on another occasion in the right
conditions, they provided wonderful views into
the Knoydart peninsula and over the South
Kintail Ridge.

200g/7oz soya mince
1 medium onion, peeled and chopped
1 spoon olive oil or margarine
1 x 126g packet of instant mashed potato

Fry the onion for a couple of minutes in the oil or margarine and then add water (1½ times the volume of mince) and bring to the boil. Stir in the soya mince and simmer for a minute. Remove from the heat and boil up another pan of water for the instant mashed potato, and make it up according to the instructions on the packet. If you only have one pan, add all the water required for both the mince and the mash at the first stage, and after simmering the mince just add the instant mash and stir well; this may not look too appetising but it's an adequate, quick energy source.

Variation
Other vegetables can be added to enhance the flavour. Alternatively the onion and oil can be omitted; this will create the simplest of all meals.

SPICY BLACK-EYED BEANS

Like all bean dishes this needs time since the beans must be soaked. In the case of a weekend climbing trip to the Dubh Loch in the Eastern Cairngorms of Scotland, this was not a problem. This is a great climbing area when the rock has dried out and there is also plenty of Munro-bagging to be had. Broad Cairn (998m/3274ft), Lochnagar (1155m/3789ft) and many others can be readily included in one weekend. There are some beautiful camping spots and doubtless a few fish to be caught in the loch.

325g/11oz black-eyed beans
1 large onion, peeled and chopped
2 cloves garlic, peeled and chopped
3 spoons olive oil

4 spoons tomato purée
**2 tsp garam masala, or ½ to 1 tsp chilli
   powder**
Half a red pepper, seeded and chopped

Soak the beans overnight or for at least eight hours. Bring to the boil, continuing for ten minutes. If you have two stoves the beans should now be simmered for a further 20 minutes while preparing the sauce. With a single stove, finish cooking the beans before preparing the sauce, then just heat them up at the end. To prepare the sauce, fry the onion and garlic in the oil for a few minutes and then add the red pepper. Alternatively add dried peppers to the beans halfway through cooking. After a couple more minutes add the garam masala or chilli powder, together with a little salt. Cook for another two minutes and add the tomato purée, cooking for a further three minutes, adding a little water to help constitute a sauce. Drain the beans and mix well with the sauce. This is quite a substantial dish and probably does not need anything to accompany it.

Variation

Add some grated cheese when mixing the beans and sauce, or simply sprinkle grated cheese on top.

SWEET & SOUR FISH

Although this recipe is ideally made with fresh (or frozen) white fish, I've also known it be adaptable to tinned fish, with anything from tuna to sardines. Some friends at the spectacular Mt. McKinley (6193m/20,320ft) base camp in Alaska created this from their limited supplies. In that instance a ready-made sauce was used; with the following sauce an extra dimension is added to the recipe, but you may have to make do with a less breathtaking backdrop.

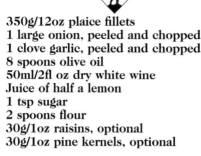

350g/12oz plaice fillets
1 large onion, peeled and chopped
1 clove garlic, peeled and chopped
8 spoons olive oil
50ml/2fl oz dry white wine
Juice of half a lemon
1 tsp sugar
2 spoons flour
30g/1oz raisins, optional
30g/1oz pine kernels, optional

Fry the onion and garlic in half the oil for a couple of minutes and then add the wine, lemon juice and sugar. Simmer for a few minutes until reduced by about a third and then add the raisins and pine kernels. Cook for a further two minutes. Either after this — or if you have a second stove, while simmering the sauce — fry the fish in the remaining oil after coating it lightly in flour. Pour the sauce over the fish and allow to stand for five minutes for the flavour to develop.

Variation
Use a tin of sardines or tuna in oil instead of the plaice. In this case add to the sauce with the raisins to allow the fish to warm through.

TUNA CORNY

An ideal one to cook if you're in a hurry, or short of fuel. A reminder of the picturesque Glen Clova to the north of Perth, a pleasant and accessible area which offers sunny rock-climbing and, at its upper end, the two Munros, Driesh (947m/3107ft) and Mayar (928m/3045ft). However my favourite hill there is a Corbett, Ben Tirran (896m/2941ft) since I climbed this on one of those magical winter days with crystal clear blue skies.

1x 225g/8oz tin tuna in oil
1 x small tin sweetcorn (optional)

1 onion, peeled and chopped (optional)
1 x 126g packet instant mashed potato

Drain the oil from the tuna into a pan and fry the onion in this for a few minutes until soft but not brown. Add the tuna to heat through, followed by the drained sweetcorn, stirring well. Remove from the pan and put to one side. Boil the required quantity of water as per manufacturer's instructions for the mashed potato. Stir in the potato powder or granules and stir well, then add the tuna mix, together with salt and pepper to taste, mixing well.

Variation
Add finely sliced cheese or some curry powder

TURKEY Á LA KING

Loch an Daimh sits between the Munros of Stuc an Lochain (960m/3150ft) and Meall Buidhe (932m/3058ft) to the west of Aberfeldy. The temptation for many is to do one of them, return to the road and make off over to the other. Far better to make a circuit of the loch and add in a couple of Corbetts, one of which is also another Meall Buidhe (910m/2985ft). Westward lies Rannoch Moor with Ben Nevis (1344m/4409ft) and the peaks around Glencoe visible on a clear day. You could even extend your trip into two days and this dish is a suggestion for the overnight camp.

255g/9oz diced turkey
115g/4oz mushrooms, sliced
1 medium onion, peeled and chopped
200ml/7fl oz milk
1 heaped spoon flour
1 spoon olive oil
1-2 spoons margarine
1 tsp oregano

Fry the onion in the oil and margarine until soft but not brown. Add the turkey and fry for another five minutes. Add the oregano and mushrooms, and perhaps a little extra margarine if the ingredients appear too dry, and fry for a further two minutes. Stir in the flour and when well absorbed, gradually add enough milk, stirring continuously, until a pouring consistency is obtained. Season to taste.

Serve with pasta or rice.

TURKEY WITH APRICOTS

This is a dish presenting an interesting mix of flavours, with a hint of sweet and sour about it. A traverse of the Grey Corries near Fort William in late spring was the scene for this meal, prepared at the bothy at the eastern end of the range. These hills provide great walking with opportunities for multi-day outings taking in many more of the Munros, and a few Corbetts, in the vicinity. However my aim is still for a ski traverse, when conditions allow.

325g/11oz diced turkey
8 dried apricots, chopped
3 shallots, peeled and sliced or 1 medium
    onion, peeled and chopped
100ml/4fl oz white wine
2 spoons natural yoghurt
Approx 100ml/4fl oz stock (or water)
1 tsp tarragon
2 spoons olive oil

Fry the shallots (or onion) lightly in oil for three minutes. Add the turkey and fry for a further five minutes. Then add the apricots along with the wine and tarragon and simmer for ten to 15 minutes. Add the yoghurt and stir this in well and allow to cook for a couple of minutes; add a little water or stock to give the sauce a pouring consistency, but ensure it is not too thin.

Serve on a bed of rice or with mashed potato. Add a green vegetable for the final touch.

Variation
Use pork as an alternative to turkey.

8

DESSERTS

D esserts are often overlooked when camping and certainly a piece of fresh fruit or some cheese is often all that is needed to round off a meal. If weight is not important then tinned fruit is a good option. One of my favourite desserts is simply to make up a packet of Angel Delight or similar, using reconstituted dried milk, and then simply add in a sliced banana. This became our staple 'pud' on a prolonged trip into the Southern Alps of New Zealand.

The dessert recipes I have included are all pretty straightforward; pancakes are probably the hardest. There are also a few desserts included in the barbecue section. Another easy one was a tip from some friends who have often toasted slices of cake, just using a pan directly over the stove to form the toaster.

BANANA CUSTARD

The traditional recipe is based on fresh bananas and custard powder made up with milk. For lightweight camping the following version is more practical. I used this on a trip into the Galloway Hills in South-west Scotland which often surprise people with their ruggedness and remote mountain feel. The walking is great and the names conjure up some interesting images — The Awful Hand Range, Round Loch of the Dungeon, the Murder Hole and so on.

**Half a 250g/8½oz packet of sun-dried
bananas**
**1 x 75g/2½oz packet instant custard
(makes 450ml/¾pt)**
2 spoons jam (optional)

Chop up the bananas and mix in the jam.
Make up the custard as per instructions on the
packet and pour over the banana.

Variation
If you can manage to carry fresh bananas this
produces a much tastier dish. Other dried fruits
such as apricot or apple can also be used.

BANANAS FLAMBÉED IN GRAND MARNIER

This is definitely my classic dessert for
camping, since it is very easy and delicious. This
developed out of a conversation one beautiful
weekend on the Isle of Skye. The dramatic and
rugged ridge of the Cuillins dominated the
skyline as the sun set and we knew we were
going to have a glorious couple of days of
scrambling. When the weather is right, Skye is
unbeatable — a bit like this recipe!

1 large or 2 small bananas, sliced
**1 spoon orange juice, or juice of a fresh
orange**
15ml (1 miniature) Grand Marnier
1 tsp sugar
1 spoon margarine

Fry the bananas gently in margarine for a
couple of minutes. Add the orange juice and stir
in the sugar until dissolved. Add the Grand
Marnier and as soon as this has heated, set light
to it to flambée the bananas. Once the alcohol has
burnt off, check if any more sugar is needed.
Serve on its own or with cream.
Do not try cooking this one inside a tent!

BLACKBERRY & APPLE

This is an ideal dessert for the early autumn when blackberries are readily available. Maybe you'll pick them at the roadside as you drive to the hills, or perhaps, as I did, while you walk through woodland on the lower slopes of the hill. In my case it was an ascent of Beinn a'Bheitir (1024m/3360ft), often known as the Ballachulish Horseshoe. On a clear day this offers magnificent views across Loch Linnhe to Mull and the Ardgour Peninsula, and is a place to savour.

**1 large cooking apple, or 2 eating apples,
    peeled, cored and sliced
1 large cupful blackberries
Greek yoghurt (optional)
Custard/milk (optional)
Sugar**

A cooking apple is preferable but if you just come across the blackberries unexpectedly, use whatever you have. Put the apple in a pan with a very little water and stew for a few minutes until beginning to go soft. Add the blackberries and stew for a few minutes more. Add sugar to taste. Serve on its own or with Greek yoghurt or custard.

FRUIT SALAD

What could be simpler than a simple fruit salad? A selection of fresh fruit can produce a wonderfully refreshing dessert on a hot day and so this is really a recipe to remind me of holidays in the southern part of France. After a day's climbing on one of the classic multi-pitch rock routes at Ailefroide in the Ecrins National Park, we returned to the village campsite, surely one of the most pleasant official campsites anywhere in the world. Temperatures had been in the 30's so a simple cold meal with some chilled white wine was nicely rounded off with this fruit salad.

Any four items from the following:
1 apple
1 pear
1 nectarine
1 orange
A handful of grapes
1 banana
2 or 3 plums
Juice of half a lemon or orange (optional)
2 spoons sugar (optional)
Greek yogurt (optional)

In its simplest form all that is necessary is to peel the orange and banana, remove the stones from the plums and the cores from the apple and pear, slice the lot and mix it all together. However, if you have more time, the flavour can be dramatically enhanced in the following way.

Some time before you want to eat, dissolve two spoons of sugar in about 200ml/7fl oz of water and bring to the boil for a few minutes. Add the lemon or orange juice and allow it to cool. Then prepare the fruit as above and add to the syrup and mix in well.

Serve with Greek yoghurt.

GROUND RICE PUDDING

Another simple pudding, and if made with dried milk it's very lightweight, perfect for a mountain marathon in fact; the one I have in mind was in the Arrochar Alps to the west of Loch Lomond, already mentioned for one of my pasta dishes. This turned out to be one of the toughest areas used for such an event. We struggled with difficulty to find our way around in the mist, even to find the summit of Ben Donich (852m/2795ft) and arrived well-soaked at the campsite. This dish certainly helped with the revitalisation process.

300ml/½pt milk
30g/1oz ground rice
1 spoon sugar
A little ground nutmeg, or cinnamon
    (optional)

Heat the milk until lukewarm and add the ground rice, sprinkling it in and stirring while continuing to cook for three minutes on a moderate heat. Add the sugar, again stirring until dissolved. Simmer for about ten minutes, stirring occasionally. When tender it is ready to serve. Sprinkle with nutmeg or cinnamon.

PANCAKES

As described in the recipe for savoury pancakes (see page 83), the easy way is to use pancake mix. However I'm also including the full recipe here. A non-stick pan is strongly recommended; another good way to cook them is if you have a barbecue with a griddle. I was walking the Routeburn Track in New Zealand when trying this out. This track must be rated as one of the top walks in the world; it has a great variety of scenery with lush rainforest and open views of more distant, spectacular snowy summits.

115g/4oz flour, 1 egg & 150ml/¼pt milk
    or 1 x 90g packet pancake mix, (or use
    part of a larger packet)
3-4 spoons jam, or some lemon juice plus
    sugar

Mix in the egg with the flour and gradually add the milk, stirring well, or make up the pancake mixture according to the manufacturer's instructions. Heat a little oil and pour in just enough mixture to cover the pan; cook until bubbles appear and then turn the pancake to cook the other side. Serve with jam or lemon juice and sugar.

PEARS IN RED WINE

The red wine seems to suggest a sunset. A dish to sample on one of those beautiful long spring evenings in the north of Scotland. I was in a very relaxed mood watching the sun go down over Loch Laxford, halfway between Ullapool and Cape Wrath. The loch is surrounded only by low hills to the west but it still gives a feeling of being in the mountains, which of course it is. Nearby to the east are the wonderful hills of Arkle (787m/2581ft) and Foinaven (911m/2989ft).

2 pears, peeled, cored and quartered
150ml/¼pt red wine
1 spoon sugar
1 cinnamon stick, or ½ tsp ground
    cinnamon
3 cloves (optional)

Place the pears in a pan with the red wine, one spoonful of sugar and some cinnamon (stick preferred). Bring gently to the boil, simmer for two minutes and then remove the pan and set it to one side, for as long as possible. If you can start this dish before preparing the main course, this is ideal. Turn the pear quarters occasionally while the dish is standing. Just before you are ready to eat it, return the pan to the stove and cook for a few more minutes. Add more sugar to taste.

For a touch of luxury serve with Greek yoghurt.

For one person use about two-thirds the quantity of wine; otherwise there is not enough to cover the pears sufficiently.

SPICED RICOTTA WITH FRUIT

Another simple dessert which I first tried while camping in the beautiful Atherton Tablelands in Queensland, Australia, not too far from Cairns. This is very much an area for bird life and I was woken in the morning by a deafening dawn chorus. Although not an ornithologist, I became quite fascinated by the great variety of birds in this part of Australia, to which I plan to return.

115g/4oz dried apricots (about 16 apricots)
1 small tub (55-85g/2-3oz) ricotta cheese
1 spoon sugar (brown if available)
¼ tsp ground cinnamon
A few mixed nuts

Mix the ricotta cheese, sugar and cinnamon together well and then stir in the apricots. Dried apricots vary considerably in moisture content; if they are not moist the flavour can be enhanced by soaking in a little water for an hour or so. Serve and sprinkle with chopped or crushed nuts.

Variation
Substitute sliced bananas instead of apricots.

SUMMER PUDDING

Friends of mine found themselves with some leftover bread and having picked plenty of bilberries and wild raspberries in Glen Clova and turned them into this excellent refreshing dessert. Glen Clova can be a sunny haven on the right day, and features good rock climbing with several good camping spots.

450g/1lb summer fruits (strawberries, raspberries, bilberries, blackcurrants, cherries)
30-55g/1-2oz sugar
About 6 slices of bread

Ideally you want a mixture of two or three different fruits for this, but just use what's available. Wash the fruit, remove stalks and stones and put them in a pan with a little sugar; cook over a gentle heat for three to five minutes until soft and remove them from the heat. Add a little more sugar if need be, but the fruit should be slightly on the tart side. If using blackcurrants, add a little water and cook these until they begin to soften before adding other softer fruits. Remove the crusts from the bread and line a pan (preferably wiped round with margarine or butter) with most of this, filling any gaps with small pieces of bread. Fill the pan with the fruit, but reserve any juice, and cover with the remaining bread.

Cover with a plate and leave in a cool place for a few hours. If the plate is small enough, put a weight such as a fist-sized stone on it for the duration of this process. Remove the plate and weight and pour over the remaining juice before serving. If you are feeling adventurous you can try turning it all out on to a large plate.

9

BREAKFAST

In summer, breakfast tends to be muesli, bread and jam along with a brew-up. However in autumn and winter I prefer to fortify myself a bit against the cold weather and a cooked breakfast is the way to do this. Bacon and egg is always a good one, perhaps with some fried bread and a sausage, the only problem being cleaning the pan afterwards. Porridge is also easy if you use a quick-cook variety.

Before even getting out of my sleeping bag on a cold morning I must have a cup of tea. To make this quickly, especially if it's been cold enough overnight to freeze a pan of water, one tip is to fill a flask with boiling water before going to bed. We've also perfected the technique of passing tea to another tent which is (just) out of reach! Put it in a 'Sigg' bottle, or a flask (if it's an unbreakable one), and throw it!

It is possible to make toast of a sort by using a pan as the toaster, but this can make a bit of a mess and I tend not to bother. Jam and honey can be transported in refillable plastic tubes which are available from some camping shops, and these are also suitable for soft margarine.

BUBBLE & SQUEAK

This is one that takes me back to my earliest days of camping. Now it is a regular favourite, perhaps in Glen Coe, a frequently visited area in winter; even in summer it often seems to have the weather for a cooked breakfast. Bidean nam

Bian (1150m/3773ft) is my favourite mountain in the area as it offers walking, climbing, scrambling and skiing. One of the routes is via the Lost Valley, which is not only interesting for its scenic properties but also has much history associated with it since it was once used as a hiding place by the clans.

Since this is made from leftover vegetables, the ingredients list is fairly imprecise. Just make sure you cook too much to eat for dinner the night before. All you need are:

A good portion of potatoes
Some green vegetables, such as cabbage
**   or sprouts, chopped**
2 spoons margarine or olive oil

Mash the potatoes and mix with the cabbage or sprouts. Season to taste and form into cakes; fry these in the margarine or oil, turning after a few minutes.

Variation
If you've eaten all the spuds at dinner you can make this with instant mash.

EGG IN THE HOLE & EGGY BREAD

These two recipes are easy ways to cook egg and bread. The first is associated with Ben Vorlich (985m/3232ft) and Stuc a'Chroin (975m/3199ft) on the south side of Loch Earn in Perthshire, a couple of good Munros with a number of climbing possibilities. From either north or south they can make a nice horseshoe and the ascent of the latter peak can have added interest in winter. I have explored many routes up them since they have now become my local hills.

2 or 4 slices bread (thick slices for egg in
**   the hole)**

2 eggs
2 spoons margarine or olive oil

For egg in the hole:
Cut a hole in each slice of bread, about 6cm/2½in across, fry on one side for a couple of minutes until just starting to brown. Turn over and put the egg into the hole; season, cover and cook gently until the egg is set, about three or four minutes. Fry the other piece of bread you have cut out at the same time. Repeat for second slice/egg.

For eggy bread:
Whisk the eggs in a pan and dip the bread into this mix, turning to coat both sides. Fry for a few minutes on each side. Continue with the next slice of bread until all the egg is used (this may take more than the four slices I suggested above).

Variation
Add some dried mixed herbs to the mix.

SCRAMBLED EGG WITH TOMATO

A simple variation on simple scrambled eggs. Unusually I decided on a cooked breakfast in the middle of summer before an ascent of that most northerly Munro, Ben Hope (927m/3041ft) near Altnaharra. The area is remote and provides good views to Ben Loyal (764m/2506ft) and Foinaven, which, although lower, are in fact more interesting. It is well worth spending as much time as possible in the far north of Scotland, exploring some of the unspoilt coastline, with its mixture of beaches and cliffs.

4 eggs
2 small or 1 large tomato, chopped
1 spoon margarine

Fry the tomatoes in the margarine until soft. Add salt and pepper and the eggs, whisking well while the mixture cooks gently. Do not allow it to become too firm before removing from the heat. The snag with scrambled egg is that it does tend to stick to the pan, so a non-stick pan is a good idea; or leave the washing up until you get home!

10

COOK-AT-HOME RECIPES

There are numerous opportunities to prepare dishes at home and take them with you. The range of possibilities is almost endless and therefore many recipes are available from a wide range of cookery books. I've included a small selection of my favourites. Stews and casseroles can also be cooked while camping but do take a long time. The time can be cut down by use of a pressure cooker or you can use the haybox cooking method as described in chapter seven (see page 63). However, if you are not walking too far it is simpler to prepare them at home and carry them in a well-sealed container.

High energy sweet dishes such as cakes and flapjacks are great to eat on the hill on a cold, wet day, or with a brew-up when you return to camp. It is possible to make a camp oven and cook a cake, and I have seen some very impressive results, even to the extent of an iced cake! However for most of us this is not practical and these are ideal things to make at home and carry in your rucksack.

Pies and pasties are a good way to make up something different for lunch and there is a whole range of possibilities, of which I have just given one simple example.

One of the most pleasant surprises I've had was a peach tart produced from a rucksack after a few wet hours walking in the dark. I thoroughly recommend the effort in preparing, and the care in transporting this, for a special occasion.

The metric/imperial conversions in some of these recipes differ slightly from those used elsewhere in order to maintain accurate proportions of the various ingredients for cakes. Use either metric or imperial, but do not mix the two in the same recipe. The quantities for the cakes are also larger than the standard two portions used elsewhere.

BEEF CASSEROLE WITH DUMPLINGS

Dumplings are a great addition to many of the casseroles of which this is one of the tastiest. Perhaps it's the shape of the dumplings, since this tends to evoke an image of the rounded mountains of the Cairngorms on a winter day. The cold weather often experienced there is well-matched by this warming dish.

**325g/11oz shoulder or other stewing
   steak
1 onion, peeled and sliced
1 carrot, sliced
300ml/½pt beef stock, or 100ml/4fl oz
   each of beef stock and beer or stout
1 bayleaf
2 spoons flour
3 spoons olive oil or margarine**

For the dumplings:

**55g/2oz self raising flour
30g/1oz suet**

Pre-heat oven to 160C/325F/Gas Mark 3

Fry the onion in the oil or margarine for a couple of minutes and then add the meat and fry for about ten minutes, turning from time to time. Stir in the flour and cook for another minute. Gradually add in the stock and/or beer stirring continuously until thickened. Add the bayleaf and carrot, then transfer to a casserole and cook in the oven for 90 minutes.

To make the dumplings mix the self-raising flour, suet and a pinch of salt with a little cold water to form a dough. Make this into two or four dumplings and place in the casserole then return to the oven for a further 30 minutes.

Serve with boiled or mashed potato.

Variation
Further vegetables such as celery or a green pepper can be added with the carrot.

LENTIL & BACON PASTIES

The pasty is of course the original packed lunch, but it has developed a long way from the Cornish miner's original. I took some on a mountain bike trip around the Coromandel Peninsula just east of Auckland, New Zealand. This is a most beautiful area, never rising very high but nevertheless remaining very hilly, giving a good workout on a bike. Take your time for the round trip from the town of Thames and stop at the wonderful beach at the northern tip of the peninsula.

> 1 x 284g/10oz packet of frozen pastry
>   (shortcrust if possible) or 150g/6oz
>   wholemeal flour and 85g/3oz butter
> 140g/5oz lentils
> 4 rashers bacon, chopped
> 350g/12oz potatoes, peeled and cut into
>   smallish pieces
> 1 medium onion, peeled and chopped
> 2 spoons olive oil
> 1 tsp garam masala or curry powder
> Milk for glazing

Pre-heat the oven to 200C/400F/Gas Mark 6

First cook the lentils. For green lentils, soak for a couple of hours and then boil in salted water for about 40 minutes; for red lentils just boil in salted water for 20 minutes without soaking. Add the potato halfway through if boiling green lentils or at the start if cooking with red lentils. While these are cooking either make the pastry (see first part of recipe for Peach Tart on page 112) or let the packet thaw out. Divide into four and roll out into pieces about 15cm/6inches square.

Fry the onion in the oil for a few minutes before adding the bacon; after another few minutes add the garam masala or curry powder (quantity can be adjusted to taste). When the lentils and potato are cooked, drain well and mash; add the onion/bacon mixture and mix together. Divide into four and place on to one half of each piece of pastry and then fold over. Push the edges together using a little milk to help join these and brush the pasties with some milk. Bake in the oven for about 20 minutes until golden brown. The pasties can be made a couple of days before they are consumed, or they can be frozen.

Variation

The bacon can be replaced with red or green pepper to produce a vegetarian pasty.

RYE BREAD

Bread is a part of the staple diet for most of us, yet after a few days most bread has gone stale. A good solid rye bread seems to last somewhat longer, and is much more durable when stuffed into a rucksack. I have therefore got in the habit of making this from time to time and taking it in to the hills.

A ski-tour taking in some of the huts around Chamonix comes to mind where there is plenty of great ski-mountaineering to be had. Although a very popular area, once away from the Haute Route it is possible to find some great touring without seeing too many people.

400g/14oz rye flour
350g/12oz wholemeal bread flour
30g/1oz lard, or 2 spoons olive oil
1 packet easy-bake yeast

Pre-heat oven to 230C/450F/Gas Mark 8

Bread is so much easier to make now that yeast is available in sachets which do not need preparation. Mix the two types of flour and rub the lard into the flour, or stir in the olive oil. Add the packet of yeast and mix before adding 450ml/¾pt lukewarm water. Mix well and knead for ten minutes to form a soft elastic dough. Leave in a warm place for about 45 minutes, until the mix doubles in size. Re-knead for five minutes and divide into two parts. Either put into two 450g/1lb bread tins, or simply shape into flat round loaves; in the latter case cut a cross in the surface to allow the tension to be released during the next stage. This stage is to let the dough rise again for 45-60 minutes in a warm place. Bake in the oven for 30-40 minutes until browned and sounding hollow when tapped. Allow to cool on a wire rack.

APRICOT & NUT LOAF

This is an easily made cake which does not have any fat added, although the nuts do mean it can hardly be called 'fat-free'. I tried this out for a climbing trip to Spain when each of us on the trip brought along a different cake — a great idea for a week's trip based around one place.

140/5oz self-raising flour, wholemeal
    preferably
115g/4oz dried apricots, chopped small
115g/4oz raisins or sultanas
55g/2oz chopped almonds or walnuts
85g/3oz soft brown sugar
1 egg
½ tsp ground cinnamon
½ tsp grated nutmeg

Pre-heat oven to 180C/350F/Gas Mark 4.

Soak apricots in 150ml/5fl oz hot water for at least six hours, or overnight. Sift the flour and mix all the dry ingredients together; add the egg and the apricots, including the water. Mix well and put into a greased or lined 450g/1lb loaf tin. Bake in the oven for 40-50 minutes. Check that a knife inserted into the centre comes out dry to indicate it is cooked. Turn out and leave to cool on a wire rack.

BANANA BREAD

A tasty and nourishing cake/bread which should keep for several days. It makes great elevenses on top of the mountain, or goes well with that first brew-up at the campsite. I was introduced to this on a day in the remote Fannich hills near Ullapool, which are one of my favourite ranges in Scotland.

115g/4oz demerara or brown sugar
55g/2oz margarine
225g/8oz wholemeal self raising flour, sifted
2 eggs
3 medium bananas

Pre-heat oven to 180C/350F/Gas Mark 4.

Cream together the sugar and margarine; add the beaten eggs and stir in the sifted flour and mashed bananas. Put into a greased or lined 450g/1lb loaf tin. Bake in the oven for 50-60 minutes. Check that a knife inserted into the centre comes out dry to indicate it is cooked. Turn out and leave to cool on a wire rack.

Variation
Add 55g/2oz chopped walnuts. Spices such as cinnamon or ginger can also be added.

FLAPJACKS

These are a tasty snack which are easy to make and ideal for mountain marathons or training runs in the hills. I took some on an epic run with some friends when we ran from Loch Lomond over Ben Lomond (974m/3195ft), Ben Venue (726m/2382ft), Ben Vane (915m/3002ft) and Ben Ledi (879m/2883ft), which must have been about 35km with over 2500m/8200ft of ascent. If I'd just been eating flapjacks this would have meant taking about 30 of them, so these were just a part of the food intake!

115g/4oz oats
90g/3½oz margarine or butter
55g/2oz brown sugar
85g/3oz golden syrup

Pre-heat oven to 190C/375F/Gas Mark 5.

Ideally you should use jumbo oats or similar which can be bought at health food shops, but this recipe also works with porridge oats; the texture obtained in the end result is slightly different.

Melt the margarine, sugar and golden syrup but do not boil. Remove from the heat and stir in the oats until well mixed. Press into a greased square cake tin or Swiss roll tin, about 18cm/7inch square for the quantity above, and bake in the oven for 25 to 30 minutes, until golden brown. Score the surface in squares and then leave to cool for about five minutes before removing from the tin and cutting right through. This makes six flapjacks of approximately 250 calories each, and they will keep for about a week in a sealed container.

Variation
Add about half a teaspoon of ground ginger or cinnamon to spice it up.

DATE & RAISIN SLICE

This travels well, keeps for several days and can be frozen. The recipe came to me from friends on a ski-touring trip on the hills around Glenshee in Perthshire. They sampled this on the summit of Glas Maol (1068m/3504ft) on a perfect day, away from the crowds on the lift-served slopes not far away, looking across the range of some 12 Munros in the area. This area is excellent for touring on Telemark skis, especially if you can arrange transport to pick you up at Loch Muick and thus make a complete traverse of the hills.

225g/8oz dates, chopped
50g/2oz raisins
2 (slightly rounded) tablespoons honey
2 tablespoons lemon juice
225g/8oz plain flour
225g/8oz rolled oats
225g/8oz margarine
85g/3oz brown sugar

Pre-heat oven to 190C/375F/Gas Mark 5.

Simmer the honey, lemon juice, dates and raisins for about ten minutes until soft, and allow to cool slightly. Meanwhile mix the oats and the flour, rub in the margarine and then add the sugar. Press half the mixture into a greased or lined square tin (20cm/8inch). It is important to press this down well or the next stage will become messy and you may not get a slice as the end result. Then spread the date/raisin mix over the oat mixture already in the pan and finally add the remainder of the oat mixture and press down gently.

Bake in the oven for 35 to 40 minutes, until golden brown on top.

Remove from the oven and cut into a dozen pieces, each of which will contain about 350 calories. Leave them in the pan until completely cooled and then remove. They will keep in a sealed container for about two weeks.

Variation
Other dried fruit such as apricots or prunes can also be used, but add a couple more tablespoons of water. I have also tried adding some banana in place of some of the dates.

APPLE CRUMBLE

An all-time favourite pudding at home for many people, this can easily be cooked in a foil tray and taken into the hills.

350g/12oz cooking apples, peeled, cored and sliced
55g/2oz butter or margarine
115g/4oz plain flour
45g/1½oz sugar plus additional sugar for apples

Preheat oven to 200C/400F/Gas Mark 6.
Stew the apples with a little water and sugar to taste. Cook for about five minutes until just soft. Meanwhile rub butter or margarine into the flour until the mixture looks like fine breadcrumbs and then stir in the sugar. Put the stewed apple into a foil tray (as you would get from a Chinese takeaway) and cover with this mixture. Bake in the oven for about 20 to 30 minutes until the top is just starting to brown. Remove and allow to cool before packing, complete with foil tray into a suitable lunch-box. Serve cold but preferably with hot (instant) custard.

Variation
Crumble can be made with most fruits, such as plums, rhubarb, apricots etc. If you are a cinnamon fan you can spice up the apple accordingly.

PEACH TART (SERVES 6)

Sounds a bit exotic for camping? Well we'd been walking for several hours on a dark, wet November evening in southern Norway and were looking forward to finding the hut. The ground was waterlogged and it was great to arrive and get settled in. After we'd had something to eat Carl said 'Wouldn't it be great if we had one of Rosie's peach tarts now?' So saying, he produced one out of his rucksack, carefully transported without damage! The scenic reward was kept for the next day when we reached the spectacular Lysefjord.

- **1 x 284g/10oz packet of frozen pastry (shortcrust if possible) or 170g/6oz plain flour (white or wholemeal) and 85g/3oz butter**
- **3 large peaches, peeled and sliced, or 1 x 800g can peaches, drained**
- **2 spoons apricot jam**
- **A little caster sugar**

Pre-heat oven to 200C/400F/Gas Mark 6.

Sift the flour with a pinch of salt into a bowl and rub in the butter until mixture looks like breadcrumbs. Add a little water, about two to three tablespoons and mix to form a soft dough. Leave this for five minutes to stand before rolling out and lining a 20cm/8inch flan dish. If using the frozen pastry, roll this out after thawing and line the tin. Prick the base with a fork and bake in the oven for 15 minutes.

Spread the jam over the pastry base and then lay on the sliced peaches and sprinkle with a spoonful of caster sugar (double the quantity if using fresh peaches). Bake for a further 20 minutes (canned peaches) or 30-40 minutes (fresh peaches) in a moderate oven (180C/350F/Gas Mark 4).

Variation

Other fruit such as apricots, plums or apples may be used. Ground cinnamon can be sprinkled over the fruit and is particularly good with apples.

11

BARBECUES & CAMP-FIRE
COOKING

A traditional barbecue is not the sort of thing you are likely to take on a backpacking trip, but disposable barbecues are widely available and are lighter (although a bit more bulky) than a stove. Just be sure that the messy remains are taken back with you! However, when car camping it is certainly quite feasible to make use of a traditional barbecue. On official campsites in some countries, notably the United States and Australia, a fireplace is common and a barbecue grid or griddle is often incorporated.

Camp-fires are a much more realistic possibility when backpacking, depending on the locality. It is most important to obey the normal rules to prevent damage to the environment. Only dead wood should be used; fires must be properly extinguished afterwards and the site of the fire should be restored to the state in which it was found and, above all, no fire should be considered if there is any declared or perceived state of fire risk.

The big advantage of a fire is that items can be baked provided they are suitably wrapped, generally in foil. If cooking in this way the fire, or at least the part of the fire where you are cooking, needs to have died down to glowing embers. If you have a grid, you can just get away with the wood still burning, but careful watching of the food is necessary.

Most of the dishes are quite simple, since there is enough to occupy you in keeping the fire or barbecue in the right state and prevent burning the food. However one of the great things about this type of cuisine is that usually everyone wants to help. With such a sociable focus the barbecue or fire is well-suited to cooking for larger numbers.

Fish can make a good barbecue dish, especially varieties such as trout, salmon or red mullet. These can either be wrapped in foil, or if you are careful you can cook direct, especially red mullet which has a tough skin to protect it.

Popular in New Zealand, but less common elsewhere, is the 'smoker'. This is a metal box of some description (various designs exist) in which you place some wood chippings, put the food on a grid above these, put on the lid and place it all on the fire or barbecue. Many different foods can be cooked in this way, but fish is especially good. Clearly this is for car camping only.

BAKED APPLES

On one particular weekend I had no preconceived plans, other than to tick off a few scattered Munros and I was approaching completion of my bagging. Steve and I ended up camped at the top end of Loch Etive in Argyll, where a stony beach provided a perfect setting for a camp-fire and an excuse for a good feed. With Ben Starav (1078m/3537ft) across the loch and the classic Etive Slabs behind us, we enjoyed perfect weather throughout the weekend.

2 (cooking) apples
2 spoons sugar (or honey)

Wash and core the apples and score the skin around their circumference. Place in foil, add the sugar or honey to the centre along with a spoonful of water and tightly wrap up in the foil.

Place in the embers, or on the barbecue, but not in too hot a place. The apples will probably take an hour to an hour and a half to cook. Test by squeezing them gently and if they seem done open up the foil to check. One advantage of apples is they can still be eaten even if not cooked right through!

Variation

Put some dried mixed fruit and cinnamon in the centre of the apples. You can substitute with eating apples if you use a variety such as Granny Smith.

BAKED POTATOES

These are always a favourite with barbecued food. It is rare to have a barbecue when camping in Scotland but one memorable September weekend I was at the campsite at Shieldaig near Torridon. After a great day of climbing and walking, and even a (very quick) dip in the sea we sat around in the warm evening sunshine, drinking and eating and watching the sun go down over the sea. Even at midnight it was pleasant with no wind at all. In the middle of the night I was awoken by a loud noise, which turned out to be the barbecue being blown across the campsite — the weather had changed!

2 large or 4 medium potatoes
Sour cream or butter (optional)

Wrap the potatoes in foil and place in the embers of the barbecue or fire for one to two hours, depending on their size and the heat. As this is always a bit of a hit and miss it's best not to be in a hurry to eat, and leave cooking the meat or fish until the potatoes are ready. There is a way round this, which is to cook the potatoes in advance at home. Then all you need to do is put them in the embers to warm up, still wrapped in foil. Cut them open and serve with sour cream, butter, or your favourite filling.

BANANAS WITH CHOCOLATE

This recalls for me the campsite at Tuolumne Meadows in Yosemite National Park, California. Bananas cooked in this way became our dessert on more than one occasion. I was there for the rock-climbing, but it is an equally superb area for walking amongst the open forests of firs surrounded by magnificent granite-domed mountains. The classic John Muir Trail starts nearby and runs for 200 miles/320km through some of the best of California's back-country; I must return to walk this again.

2 large bananas
1 x 55g/2oz bar chocolate, plain or milk

The bananas should be reasonably firm, but certainly not green. Leave the bananas in their skins and make four cuts, lengthways, at different points. Push in a couple of squares of chocolate into each slit and wrap the bananas in foil. Place on the barbecue, or in the embers of the fire, for about five to ten minutes, until the banana is beginning to soften. Open the foil and check that the chocolate has just melted; if necessary return to the heat for a few minutes more.

GARLIC BREAD

Ideally this should be made with real French bread, but it is still quite possible with imitations, or indeed almost any bread if that's all you can get. I used bread of the right type while camped at the Grand Canyon in Arizona. This is certainly as spectacular as expected, but the problem is the huge number of people who seem to be absolutely everywhere. If you walk right down into the canyon this changes markedly, and while you will never have the place to yourself, it is certainly much more relaxing than at the top. Despite the crowds you should not miss seeing the sunset from one of the popular viewpoints.

1 French stick
2 cloves garlic, peeled and chopped very
   fine
1-2 spoons margarine
1 tsp chopped herbs (optional)

Mix the margarine, garlic and herbs well. Cut the bread across into slices but do not cut through the bottom crust. Spread the margarine on one side of each of these cuts. Wrap in foil and place on the barbecue or in the embers of the fire. Check from time to time to prevent it burning. The bread is ready when the margarine has melted and the bread is warm. This will probably take five to ten minutes.

HAMBURGERS

Some good Aussie meat made these excellent hamburgers, and I probably had a bigger portion than this. I was paying a visit to Ayers Rock (867m/2843ft) in the very centre of Australia. It looked just like a picture postcard, but I was not entirely prepared for the crowds. Climbing it at first light to catch a beautiful sunrise, we were joined by hundreds of Japanese, most of them wearing white gloves, a bizarre item of clothing in the circumstances. The view across to the Olgas, plus a vast desert plain was wonderful.

350g/12oz minced lean beef
1 medium onion, peeled and chopped
1 egg, beaten
1 spoon chopped herbs (optional)

Mix all the ingredients together, and season

with salt and pepper. Divide into four equal amounts and press these well into burgers. Cook on the barbecue for about three to five minutes on each side according to the heat and taste. (The barbecue needs to be hot to seal in the juices.)

Variation
Add about 55g/2oz grated cheese to the ingredients.

LAMB CHOPS

Fresh tender lamb chops make superb barbecue food and it was excellent lamb I sampled in the Snowy Mountains which lie on the boundary of Victoria and New South Wales. These are beautiful mountains, mostly covered with eucalyptus and plenty of wildlife. The higher parts are above the tree-line and include Australia's highest peak, Mount Kosiusko (2228m/7310ft), and one of the country's main ski areas.

4 or 6 lamb chops, depending on size
1-2 spoons olive oil
1 spoon chopped rosemary (optional)

Wipe the chops with olive oil and sprinkle a little rosemary on to each one; press in the rosemary gently, so it stays in place when you turn the chops and repeat for the other side. Barbecue for about four minutes on each side, according to taste.

Variation
If the meat is not as young and tender as you would like, and you have the time, it is well worth marinading the meat for a few hours before cooking. Make the marinade by mixing:

150ml/¼pt red wine
75ml/3fl oz olive oil
1 spoon chopped rosemary or about ten
    juniper berries
1 small onion, peeled and sliced
1 clove garlic, peeled and crushed
Seasoning.

MARSHMALLOWS

Hardly a recipe, but these are a great addition at the end of a meal, while sitting round the campfire, chatting and drinking coffee. We were hooked on these on our climbing trip in the States. California's biggest ski area, Mammoth, has relaxing walking through magnificent pine forests, with small lakes scattered throughout the area. Given more time we could have linked up with Yosemite on the other side of the Sierra Mountains.

1 packet marshmallows

Peel the end of a reasonably long stick and use this as a toasting fork. Place a marshmallow on the end and hold near the source of heat, turning occasionally. As the marshmallow starts to melt it is ready to eat, but be careful not to burn yourself!

Variation
Instead of drinking coffee intersperse the eating of marshmallows with a wee dram.

STEAK AND ONIONS

Once again a dish that could hardly be easier. This can be a bit expensive in Britain or Europe, but in the United States or 'down under', steak comes at about a quarter of the price that it is in the UK. For this reason it was more often on the menu there and it is another reminder of a great couple of weeks at Tuolumne Meadows in Yosemite National Park. The weather was warm and sunny every day, though cold at night, and the steaks were consumed along with some of the local Californian wine.

2 steaks, each around 200g/7oz (or
bigger if you want)
1 large onion
1-2 spoons oil or margarine

The best cut of meat for this is probably porterhouse, sirloin or rib-eye. The latter is especially good for a barbecue, due to the fat which it carries.

Slice the onions into rings and fry in a little oil or margarine until slightly brown. If there is no flat griddle, the onions should be cooked in a pan. Put the steaks on the barbecue and after about 30 seconds turn them so that both sides are sealed. Reduce the heat a little and fry on each side until cooked to your taste. Timing for this is always a bit tricky and depends on how people like their steak done. About a minute on each side for a half-inch thick steak will produce a rare steak and four or five minutes per side will produce a medium done steak. This does however depend on the temperature, the cut etc.

Variation
Rub freshly ground black pepper into the steak before cooking.

Steak can also be cooked in a pan over a camping stove; in this case it's best to cook the onions first and you'll need a bit more oil for the steaks. You may need to cook one at a time unless you have a big pan.

12

DRINKS

There are a few ways of adding a bit of variety to drinks. There's a large selection of herbal teas now readily available and these make a pleasant change, especially from tea made with dried milk.

A glass or mug of mulled wine is another pleasant drink after a cold day out. Coffee, or tea for that matter, can be livened up with a tot of whisky or brandy. Alcohol and hillwalking should never be enjoyed at the same time, but a warming nightcap is a very pleasant way to end a satisfying day. I'll just give a couple of simple recipes for different types of mulled wine; the Austrian classic glühwein and a Norwegian drink, gløgg. The latter can also be used to make a warming non-alcoholic drink.

These recipes are based on a bottle of wine for convenience, but if there are just two of you it is probable you will want reduce the quantity, perhaps using the remainder of the bottle to have with your meal.

GLÜHWEIN

One of the first times I made glühwein for myself was for a day at Glenshee ski slopes. Although skiing in Scotland is not always reliable, this day was superb. Not only were the skies blue and the weather warm, but the snow was dry and the cover was extensive. We walked up above the lifts for a picnic and it was pleasant just to sit around without a jacket, supping the glühwein and eating some Christmas cake.

1 x 750ml bottle red wine
1 large stick cinnamon
About 8 cloves
½ tsp grated nutmeg
1 slice of an orange (optional)
A little sugar to taste

Put all ingredients except the sugar in the pan and heat slowly. Keep almost at simmering point for five to ten minutes to allow the flavour of the spices to be developed. It is best to keep it covered while doing this. Add sugar to taste — the amount depends on the wine used — but add it gradually since the change from being too dry and harsh to becoming over-sweet occurs very quickly.

GLØGG

As far as I know you can only purchase gløgg in Scandinavia, and Norway in particular. We were doing some gentle ski-touring on the Hardanger plateau based on the small village of Ustaoset, near to the better known resort at Geilo. Although much of the terrain is relatively flat and ideally suited to touring on Telemark skis, there are also spectacular 350m/1150ft cliffs, which have interesting gullies with potential for steep skiing.

1 x 750ml bottle red wine
1 bottle gløgg (see text)
55g/2oz raisins
A few pieces of lemon peel
1 spoon chopped blanched almonds
125ml (1 glass) brandy (optional)

No doubt there will be instructions on the bottle but if you don't read Norwegian here is my (rough) understanding. The ratio of gløgg to wine (plus brandy) is usually one to two, so check the size of the bottle as it may well be half a litre, in which case do not use it all. Heat the gløgg with the raisins and lemon peel to boiling point. Add the wine, almonds and brandy and heat through. Remove the lemon peel and serve.

GLØGG (NON-ALCOHOLIC)

1 litre carton apple juice
1 bottle gløgg (as previous recipe)
55g/2oz raisins
1 spoon chopped blanched almonds

Heat the apple juice with the raisins and almonds until boiling. Add the gløgg and serve hot.

APPENDIX A

THIS gives information on fuels, how they are named in some different parts of the world, their availability and where to purchase them. I have included what information I have even if it is incomplete, in the hope that it will be of some help.

Country	Methylated Spirits	Gas	Paraffin	(Unleaded) Petrol[1]	Coleman Fuel
Argentina			Parafina or kerosen	Nafta	Nafta balance
Australia		(Camping) gas	Kerosene	(Unleaded) petrol	Shellite
Chile			Parafina or kerosen	Bencina	Bencina blanca *Hardware stores*
France	Alcool à brûler *Most supermarkets*	(Camping) gaz *Outdoor shops, supermarkets*[2]	Pétrole	Essence (sans plomb)	Essence C
Germany	Brennspiritus *DIY stores, some supermarkets*	(Camping) gas *Outdoor shops*	Paraffin	Benzin (bleifrei)	ColemanBrennstof or rein Benzin
Italy	Alcool/Spirito da ardere *Camping shops*	(Camping) gas	Kerosene/Olio di paraffina *Camping shops*	Benzina (senza piombo)	
New Zealand			Kerosene *Garages*	(Unleaded) petrol	White spirit/Shellite *Readily available at most garages*
Norway	Rodsprit *Garages, DIY stores*	Gass *Garages, Camping shops*	Parafin *Garages*	Blyfri bensin	Not available
Switzerland	For names see France/Germany/Italy *Supermarkets*		Chemists		*Some outdoor shops (uncommon)*
UK	Methylated Spirits *Chemists*	Gas *Most outdoor shops*	Paraffin *Some garages*	(Unleaded) Petrol	Coleman fuel *Specialist outdoor shops*
USA		Camping gas *Outdoor stores*	Kerosene	(Unleaded) gas	Coleman fuel, White gas *Supermarkets*

[1]If low octane petrol is available, this is preferable to unleaded.
[2]Coleman type limited to specialist outdoor shops.

APPENDIX B
SOME USEFUL WEBSITES

FOR INFORMATION ON STOVES AND FUELS:

www.primus.se/konsument/consumer_e.htm
www.msrcorp.com/home.asp
www.optimus.se/products/

FOR OBTAINING INGREDIENTS:

www.tesco.com

INDEX

With thanks to...

Roy, for everything you have done for me and my mom over the years and for becoming my true father...

Sue, for putting up with me and all my strange ways all these years. 25 and counting... xxxx

Geoff for being a great friend.

Liam O'Connell

All the people who have inspired me over the years. The support from my fantastic family and friends, and to you for buying this book. If reading this book helps just one person change their life for the better, then it has all been worth it!

Steve Lilley

Foreword

A long time ago, in a strange and dark world far beneath the earth, there lived four little devils who stoked the fires of hell. It was hard work, but most of the time they enjoyed what they did, after all it was a job, and these days beggars can't be choosers.

The devils were in many ways just like you and me; they had their strange quirks, their strengths and weaknesses, their hopes and their worries.

Life had returned to something like normal in the days and months following the little devils' discovery of the new fuel for the fire. The new fire had helped them regain their motivation and sense of purpose.

They had gone back to their normal familiar routine – do you remember it?

Wake up, go to work, work hard, go home...
Wake up, go to work, work hard, go home...

The devils were determined that they would never let their fire go out again!

But they were about to find out that life's many twists and turns can sometimes lead to a very dark place indeed. A place that nobody wants to go to, even though the temptation can be almost too much to resist!

I have often heard it said that the simple things are the most important. Perhaps we all need reminding of that from time to time, and the devils are no different.

Why don't I introduce them to you?

Sparky

A creative soul, Sparky is always coming up with new ideas. He loves having fun and grasping the many opportunities that life brings. Sparky has a positive, "can do" attitude, is fast thinking and a bit quirky. Some people might say he is a little sensitive and doesn't like criticism, but then, who does?

Oxy

Oxy is keen to get things done. He is very good with his hands and is always the first to get stuck in when something needs to be finished. He usually sees the bright side of life, and would rather take action and complete a task than sit around talking about it all day. Some people might say Oxy is rigid and lives by rules and regulations, but that might be a bit harsh.

Diesel

A really deep thinker, Diesel is sound and reliable. You can always depend on him in a crisis. He will listen to both sides of an argument and make his own judgement. Some people might say he can be negative, a glass half-empty sort of person. But is that really the case, or is it just the thoughtful look on his face?

Stubbo

Stubbo has seen it all before. He tends to think that everything always goes wrong for him and he has a negative attitude to life in general. He doesn't like change and prefers things to carry on just the same as always. Some people might say he is one of life's victims... read on and make up your own mind!

Now, let's catch up with the little devils to find out what they have been getting up to, and see what new changes have happened in their lives.

The Fire Philosophy

Chapter 1

It had been another long and tiring day at the furnace but as Sparky strolled home, he had a sudden and unexplained urge to go off in a different direction for a change.

He had often wondered which way some of the other caverns and dark passageways led, and it wouldn't hurt to explore them for a few minutes, would it?

So, instead of going right along his usual path, he turned directly left at a fork in the road and headed into the darkness. He wasn't sure what he'd find but for some reason that night he didn't care, something was telling him to do something different, to try something new.

As he walked along he was excited at what he might find. He remembered the last time he had set out on an adventure like this with Diesel and Oxy, when they had finally found their new fire!

That was a long time ago now and all the devils had become settled into their old routines and were quite happy – although he *had* noticed that Diesel was acting strangely lately and seemed to be in a bit of a dream world. As for Stubbo, he hadn't seen him since that time at the old furnace when he was just sitting there waiting and waiting for his fire to come back to life.

Sparky had been walking for a while now and decided he should be going back home. He stopped for a moment to think, propping himself up against a rock that jutted out into the passageway. He had learnt a lot over the last few years, but then life is a constant journey and we are always learning.

As Sparky pondered on his thoughts, he leaned back further against the rock. Suddenly, there was a huge crash! He stumbled backwards through a hole that had opened up in the rock face. He was stunned for a few seconds, then slowly began to make out a narrow, low passageway in the darkness ahead. He looked behind him; he could see that somebody had tried to block the hole up and disguise it so no-one would find the entrance.

As inquisitive as ever, Sparky began to crawl through the passageway. Then he saw it! At first he thought it was just a big rock, but as he got closer he began to make out the shape of an old chest. He pulled the chest out of the passageway and stared at it. Finally, he opened it and pulled out a dusty old scroll. Through the light of his torch he could just about see the words – '*The Fire Philosophy*' – inscribed on it.

Cautiously, Sparky untied the scroll and began to read the handwritten words.

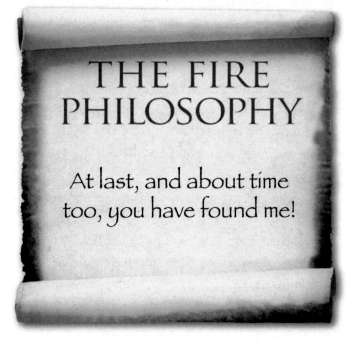

THE FIRE PHILOSOPHY

At last, and about time too, you have found me!

If you hadn't decided to do something different and go a new way home tonight, you would have never discovered me and the opportunities I bring. And that would have been your loss.

These words are going to prove very useful to you and your friends. They are simple lessons and truths that have long been established, but are sometimes easily forgotten. You are the messenger of 'The Fire Philosophy', and you have been chosen to learn and share them with your friends and family.

Sparky stared in amazement. Why had he been chosen? What did it mean? He could see that there were many more words written on the scrolls, perhaps he would find the answers there? Well, let's find out shall we?

Chapter 2

It had been an interesting few months since Diesel had found the new fire with Sparky and Oxy. At first everything had been great. He had got his debts under control and was making regular payments. He was even enjoying his work at the furnace again and spending time with his friends and family.

But as time passed he could slowly feel his personal fire beginning to burn a little less brightly. It was hard to keep up with the payments and try to enjoy himself at the same time. He knew what was important to him, but he was struggling to maintain his motivation and energy.

In fact, if the truth be told, he had been struggling so much that he had begun to drink. Not much at first – just a pint on the way home from work. He found it a great way to relax. And if we are honest, we all need a way to relax from time to time. The fast-paced modern world we live in can sometimes drain us and confuse us all. It's not unusual to feel down sometimes and lack motivation, is it?

But one pint turned into two, and then eventually three, and then...! Well, that was the problem – he knew he was drinking too much and it was affecting his attitude and his relationship with his family. He had become really moody and irritable.

He was beginning to feel not at his best at work, and sometimes it was a struggle to get up in the morning. The crazy thing was that he knew what was happening to himself, but he just couldn't stop it. He enjoyed a drink and a chat with his friends and the relief it gave him from the pressures of everyday life, but he knew that he was in danger of losing control, of losing everything! He was making an effort and he knew that at the end of the day it was up to him, it was *his* choice. Still he was finding it very difficult, and sometimes he could feel himself slipping deeper and deeper towards the darker side of life. He had seen a glimpse of it and it was a place he was determined never to go.

He knew he needed help but wasn't sure who to turn to. Then suddenly it came to him... he should speak to his old friend Sparky. Without hesitation he reached for his phone and called him.

After a few moments it rang with a strange chiming sound, then Sparky answered, "Hello?"

"It's me," said Diesel, "I think I might need your help again."

"That's weird," said Sparky, "because I've just been reading something I found yesterday and I really wanted to tell you about it. In fact, the weird thing is, I want to tell as many people about it as possible."

"What on earth is it?" Diesel asked, intrigued.

"The Fire Philosophy!" exclaimed Sparky. "I'm on my way!"

9

Chapter 3

When Sparky arrived at Diesel's place, he could see immediately that he was in a bad way. He looked washed-out and exhausted. His eyes seemed hollow and had lost their sparkle. Diesel looked older too... much older.

Diesel started to tell Sparky his troubles and how his drinking was spiralling out of control. He had always been able to control it in the past. It had been something he enjoyed, a way to forget his troubles and help him · relax. But now drink was beginning to take over and his whole life was starting to revolve around alcohol. The stupid thing was the drink didn't even seem to help him any more, it just added to his worries and anxieties.

Diesel knew he was no longer the person he used to be. His relationship with his family was suffering badly and he didn't seem to have time for anything any more, apart from drinking. He was miserable, bad-tempered, but most of all, he was sad.

Sparky looked at this friend and took a deep breath. "This is what I wanted to tell you about. I found these strange scrolls on my way home the other day and I think the words might be able to help you."

He began to read the words written on the Fire Philosophy...

THE FIRE PHILOSOPHY

Discovery

It takes a brave person to admit that they need help and the first step is to recognise it. You have already found me and my simple truths, now you must be brave and discover your true self. Look for the person that is hidden deep beneath the many complex layers of modern life.

Take some time to find the person that you used to be, the person you can be again.

Only you can decide to change things, only you can make the choice to take a different path in your life.

Ask yourself what is important to you and have the courage to make the change.

My words can guide you but it is your actions and determination that will truly help you discover your real self.

Sparky slowly put the scroll down.

Diesel looked at him anxiously. "I understand the words," he said, "but I have tried to change before and I just can't. I can do it for so long and then I just give in. Words are not enough on their own, I don't know if I have the strength to do this, Sparky."

"I know you can do it," encouraged Sparky. " Anybody can go off the rails, we all have demons. Sometimes we just need reminding of what we really want from life."

"Just give it a chance," he continued. "Think about it and decide what you really want. I will help in any way I can, but you have got to do it for yourself."

Diesel looked into Sparky's eyes and said, "I will try. I will give it a go, but this might be my last chance and I'm really frightened... I don't know if I can do it... "

Sparky knew that there were many more words of wisdom written in the scrolls of the Fire Philosophy, and he wanted to share them with as many people as possible.

Diesel was in a terrible state and Sparky wondered if it was too late to help him. However, he wasn't going to give up that easily. He decided to go and find their other good friend Oxy – he was sure he would be able to help.

Chapter 4

Oxy had been busy since finding the new fuel for the fire, very busy indeed. The shock of his old fire going out and losing his job had reminded him of what was really important to him in his life. Never again would he take for granted the important everyday things that were all around him. Finding his new fuel and motivation had helped him appreciate the simple things... his wife and family, his friends, walking his dog Flame in the countryside, and just enjoying the uncomplicated delights that nature gives us every day.

In fact sometimes he wondered if he was losing the plot, going soft in his old age, but then he really enjoyed what he was doing. He had always been happier when he was busy doing something, but now every spare minute he had he was out in his garden growing vegetables and tending to his plants. He had even starting keeping his own chickens and counting the eggs that they laid for him each day.

When Sparky arrived at Oxy's place he saw him in the garden on his knees and quickly made his way over.

"Hi!" he called. "Long time, no see... and what the devil are you doing down there?"

"Oh, hello," Oxy replied. "I'm just collecting the eggs that my hens have laid. It keeps me busy. Helps me to relax and chill out a bit... and I tell you what... you can't beat them poached on toast!"

Oxy explained to Sparky that he had learnt a lot since finding his new motivation and fire again. He was really enjoying the simple things in life once more, the things that were really important to him.

Sparky immediately began telling Oxy all about Diesel and his troubles and how he desperately needed their help.

"Diesel could do with talking to you," he said. "He needs all the help he can get."

"Oh, and there's another thing I need to tell you," he added. "The other day I stumbled on these strange scrolls and the weird thing is they seem to be guiding me and making me read them to my friends."

Sparky reached into his bag, pulled out another scroll, and began to read the words of the Fire Philosophy...

THE FIRE PHILOSOPHY

Simplicity

The simple things in life are often the most important. In this complicated, fast-paced and stressful world we live in, sometimes you need to take a deep breath and just Stop!
Take time to open your eyes wide and see the amazing things that are all around us.

Ask yourself this question, what is the most important thing to you in your life?

Simplicity

Go on then, take your time, think about it and write it down...

Often something bad or significant has to happen to us before we finally realise the simple truth that life is an ongoing journey. Why wait for that one moment – when every twist and turn along life's path is a chance to appreciate the reason why we are here in the first place?

Remember to share these thoughts with others who need reminding of life's simple truths!

Oxy looked straight at Sparky. "I don't know why you found this philosophy, or what exactly it means," he said, "but I do know something, we need to find Diesel as quickly as we can. Come on, let's go..."

22

Chapter 5

Diesel had been doing a lot of thinking in the days following his talk with Sparky. A lot of thinking indeed! He hadn't managed to stop drinking yet, but he knew he was in a very dark place and this was his last chance, he had to do something – and fast!

One morning, after a particularly heavy night, he got up and took a look in the mirror. He didn't like what he saw staring back at him at all. There was a face there that looked something like his own, yes, but it was wrinkled, bloated and tired.

He knew that if he carried on with his same old ways, soon that face would be looking even older and more worn out. In fact, one day, there might not even be a face there to look back at him at all! If he didn't stop now there would be no turning back.

Suddenly he was interrupted from his thoughts by a loud knock on the door. It was Sparky and Oxy.

He let them in and Oxy couldn't tell him quickly enough about his new simple lifestyle and what a positive difference it had made to him. Sparky couldn't contain himself and blurted out the words from the "Simplicity" Fire Philosophy, mentioning the simple truths about not waiting for something really bad to happen before changing your life for the better.

Diesel looked at them both wearily. "I know I need to change," he said. "I have nearly made up my mind to change, but there is just something stopping me from making up my mind to change for good."

With that, Sparky felt strangely compelled to pull another scroll from his bag and read the words of the Fire Philosophy...

THE FIRE PHILOSOPHY

Opportunity

Opportunity is always there for the people who look for it. But you have to really look hard for it, that is the secret.

Read these words out loud...

Opportunityisnowhere

Opportunity is nowhere

Perhaps that is the way you read it the first time. No matter how hard some people look they can never see it.

Can you see it? Look closer. Try reading it again...

Opportunityisnowhere
Opportunity is now here

Can you see it now? Yes? Good. Then recognise that change can bring opportunity. But now you have seen it, it is just as important to do something about it. Opportunity without action is pointless.

Take this opportunity to change for the better and remember to tell as many people as possible about the simple truths of the Fire Philosophy.

Discovery – Simplicity – Opportunity

Go on now, don't delay, seize the moment!

As soon as Sparky had put down the Fire Philosophy, a look of understanding came over Diesel's face.

"I think I am getting it," he said. "First of all discover the real you, then concentrate on the simple, important things in life, and then take the opportunities that come along. It's common sense really, but when we are in a particularly difficult and dark place, we sometimes need reminding of it."

Oxy agreed. "Yes," he said, "but have you noticed that the words of the Fire Philosophy always mention sharing the simple truths with your friends?"

"There is somebody we've forgotten who needs our help really badly... Stubbo!" he shouted. "We must find Stubbo!"

Chapter 6

In the days following the little devils' discovery of their new fire and motivation, a rumour went around the caverns that not everything had worked out well for every devil. It was said that Stubbo still went to the old furnace day after day, month after month, just sitting there staring sadly into the cold, dark ashes of the furnace. Waiting and waiting for the fire to spark back into life and for things to go back to the way they used to be. Sitting and staring, waiting and waiting...

Only this was no mythical rumour. This was the harsh reality of Stubbo's life. He hadn't told his friends and family the truth about what had happened and every morning he continued with the same old routine, slowly making his way to the old redundant furnace.

Stubbo wanted to think that nothing had changed in his world; he wanted to believe that if he continued to do what he always did then, as if from nowhere, the fire would come back into his life.

When Sparky, Diesel and Oxy finally arrived at the old furnace, they were dismayed to see Stubbo hunched over the damp remains of the fire.

They told him everything that had happened – their discovery of the new fire and the simple truths of the Fire Philosophy. But Stubbo didn't say a word. He remained still and silent and wouldn't even look them in the eyes.

Diesel remembered the words of the Fire Philosophy and told Stubbo what had helped him face his demons. Three simple words...

Discovery – Look for the real person inside you

Simplicity - Appreciate the simple, important things

Opportunity – Take the opportunities that life brings

But it was no good. Stubbo didn't move, didn't say a word, he just kept staring gloomily into the dark where his fire had once been.

Sadly, the three devils began to walk out of the furnace. When they were a little distance away Sparky said, "There are no more scrolls of the Fire Philosophy left in my bag. There is nothing left to guide us."

"No, but at least we have tried to help Stubbo," replied Oxy. "Some people will never change, they're just so stuck in their ways."

"But perhaps that's one of the main points of the Fire Philosophy," offered Diesel. "It is better to have tried and failed to help somebody, than to not have tried at all. If it wasn't for your help and the simple truths of the Fire Philosophy," he went on, "I could have easily gone over to the dark side. And seeing Stubbo like that has made me realise, once and for all, that I never want to let my life go off the rails again."

"It can happen to the best of us," said Sparky, "we just have to keep our eyes wide open..."

Strangely enough, taking into consideration what Sparky had just said, if they'd looked behind them they would have noticed that Stubbo had moved. He had uncurled himself from his ball of desperation and was sitting upright.

There was a different look on his face. It wasn't obvious at first, but if you looked harder you could see the beginnings of a faint smile and a glimmer of hope in his eyes...

It is better to have tried and failed to help somebody, than to not have tried at all.

The Fire Philosophy

Chapter 7

I expect you are all wondering what happened next in the lives of the little devils? Well, it is quite simple really; well, fairly simple anyway; let me explain.

Diesel managed to kick his drinking habit for good. He is often heard talking over a coffee about the simple truths of the Fire Philosophy, and the help his friends gave him to change his ways – he would be forever grateful to them. He was back to the person he used to be, much more caring and considerate. Yes, he has his moments, but then we're only human aren't we? Well, in a 'little devil' sense of the word... you know what I mean...

Oxy carried on living the simple life, tending to his chickens and his garden, and concentrating on what was really important to him, his family and friends. He does a mean omelette by the way!

Stubbo? Hmmm... Stubbo. As far as I know, he still goes to the same old ashes of the fire every day and waits and waits for his fire to come back. But it never will, will it?

But what about Sparky? Well, Sparky is doing fine! Having fun and enthusing about life in general, and still sharing the words of the Fire Philosophy with as many people as possible. There is one thing though (I think you should know) that he hasn't told the other devils.

When he got home after finding Stubbo, he found tucked away at the bottom of his bag, one final scroll of the Fire Philosophy. This is what it said...

THE FIRE PHILOSOPHY

You might be wondering why you were chosen to share the simple truths of the Fire Philosophy. Was it fate, luck or simple coincidence that you found me?

Perhaps none of these at all. But remember, I have never named you personally in any of the words written here.

I had the faith and belief that you would share my simple truths with as many people as possible.

Without faith and belief in others we have nothing, we are nothing!

Thank you, enjoy your life!

Discovery
Look for the real person
inside you

Simplicity
Appreciate the simple,
important things

Opportunity
Take the opportunities
that life brings

Meanwhile, up in the real world...

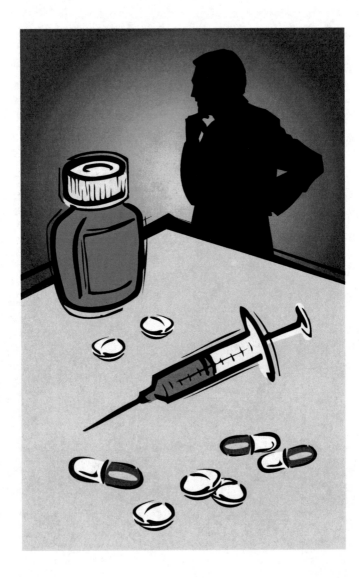

Chapter 8
James' story

James took his first drug at the age of 14. Unfortunately for him and his family this was to be just the start of an ongoing nightmare.

James is from a stable, middle-class family, has three sisters and "never wanted for anything materially or emotionally". He finished school with 6 GCSEs and had a promising career as a footballer ahead of him. But James, as he puts it, "had certain needs". He craved significance, always wanted to be the best, show off and push things to the limit. There was something missing in his life and he was determined to find it.

It was a normal weekend for James following a hard week's work as a metal finisher, and he was looking forward to going out and having a laugh with his friends.

Only James' "normal" weekend was anything but normal, and probably something that you and I will never experience in our lives! Let me explain...

Friday

12:30pm   Finish work early and home to freshen
           up and get changed.

1:30pm   Meet friends in the pub for a few beers.

5:30pm   Feeling a little tipsy and tired, take 'speed' to
           liven up, then more beers.

7:30pm   Ecstasy and 'coke', not the fizzy kind, more
           speed and drink.

11:30pm   Go to club, Es and whatever drug takes fancy.

Saturday

6:00am   Leave club with random people, pilled out of
           head and smoke cannabis.

12:00pm   Finally get head down and sleep.

6:00pm   Back to pub and repeat routine as above –
           alcohol, speed, ecstasy, coke, cannabis,
           club, crash out!

Sunday   More of the same but an early finish and a few
           drinks to see the weekend off!

James was happy with his life and managed to hold down a job and a relationship, that is until his drug habit began to spiral out of control.

One relatively quiet weekend, after years of coping with this routine, he was with a few friends drinking a 24-crate of lager and taking speed, when somebody suggested that they knew something that would help with the depressing feeling of the drug comedown.

About an hour later, after what James likes to call a "camping trip", on a bus to Alum Rock, Birmingham, he was sitting in the toilets of the pub experiencing his first life-changing hit of heroin.

"It was when heroin put her warm arms around me, it solved problems I didn't even know I had. It's that lovely feeling that you get when you are between sleep and waking up, all your troubles are washed away."

James explains that heroin was the answer to his all his "special needs". His troubles, worries and anxieties were washed away. But this new, so-called "nice" drug, was to lead to the most terrible and darkest days of his life.

As his addiction grew, he lost his girlfriend and his job, and began to steal from his family. "We rob the people we are closest to, if it wasn't nailed down you took it. I did anything to feed my habit."

He started to shoplift and was kicked out of his home by his parents. After years of sofa-surfing and the police constantly turning up on his doorstop, his heroin habit was now totally out of control. "The shops closed at five o'clock but my need for drug money didn't just stop at five. We started to burgle houses and take anything we could to fund our addiction."

At one point James woke up in a hospital bed surrounded by four policemen; he had overdosed on heroin while in the cells on remand. On another occasion he was told he had died three times and been resuscitated. He was suffering from pneumonia and septicaemia, and the sack around his heart had stopped functioning properly. As soon as he could, James ripped the tubes from his body and scored heroin.

The nightmare continued. He was living in a flat with no toilet, gas or electricity. He was urinating in one corner and smoking crack in the other. When he was finally arrested and sentenced to 15 months for burglary he was eight stone, his teeth were rotten, and he hadn't washed for months.

But even in prison he was able to maintain his heroin habit once a week.

When he was released he managed to get a job roofing, but he was soon laid off and he needed money to maintain his addiction. He didn't want to start robbing again so he made the clinical decision to become a drug pusher.

It started small at first but quickly grew. "It was at this point that something started to change inside of me. I'd had enough... enough of everything... the highs, the lows, the hurt. A drug that had once given me confidence, belief and identity, had drained me of every last ounce of my self-respect and pride."

"One day, I was selling a bag of heroin to somebody when he told me he had just sold his son's toys to pay for the hit."

"This was the moment that I put down my arrogance and put up my hand and asked for help. It had to stop; I went home and pleaded to my mum and dad to take me back."

Luckily for James, he lived in a county that had two rehabilitation centres and he followed a holistic approach. While he was beginning a course of methadone he met Dave, who was in recovery. "Dave had a similar background to me, but he had a life and I wanted one as well. He suggested going to abstinence-based rehab and it was the hardest thing I have ever done in my life."

"When I had finished the 18-week course, I sat down with a group of friends and thought of Dave. He had been the person who had motivated me and inspired me to change my life. We decided that we wanted to make a huge impact on drug rehabilitation treatment today."

James is now 36 years old and he has been clean of drugs and alcohol for 23 months.

He is chair of RIOT, Recovery Is Out There, and a service-user coordinator giving people the opportunity to recover from serious drug addiction.

As I look at James, it is impossible to see the shell of a man he used to be. He is healthy and full of energy and passion. He is literally bursting to help others change their lives.

"I am a totally different person now. I have learnt such a lot and want to share it with others. It's not about me any more; it's about the people out there in the madness. If we can help one person then our job is done."

"I get quite emotional when I think about life. Only the other day I was looking at a full moon and thinking – 'How beautiful is that?' – when for 20 years all I looked at was the ground."

"I love just waking up in the morning and appreciating the simple things in life. I have always made plans; now I just want to roll with life, take the rough with the smooth, and enjoy the moment and the people around me. I want to learn from my past and give something back to my family and my girlfriend. I even have a mortgage and a car now!"

"My work is no longer a job, it is a vocation. We are going into schools warning people about drug misuse. We are placing recovered drug addicts at all points of recovery to give them the opportunity to see that they *do* have a choice, they *can* change their lives. We are even opening a café for service-users with the Burton Addiction Centre, and partnering with local community organisations. I want to take our model nationally now."

James is a truly inspirational person. He has been to a very dark place, but at one critical moment in his life he made the choice to change for ever, for good. Now he is committed to helping as many people as possible and I have a feeling his amazing journey is only just starting.

Let's leave James with the final words.

"Don't judge people by what they are, but what they can be."

Thanks for your time, James...

Thoughts from the flames!

- It is never too late to change your life

- Learn from your own life experiences and help others

- Enjoy the simple things and appreciate every day

- Look for the good in people and give them the opportunity to succeed

Chapter 9
Owen's story

It was 22nd February 2009 – a bright Sunday – at precisely 10:21am, when Owen's entire life would change for ever.

He had spent a fun night with his girlfriend Laraine at a friend's house and they had slept in after enjoying some great food, and perhaps a little too much wine.

When he got up he struggled to put on his glasses and felt fuzzy headed... "Must be the alcohol," he told himself. Then he had trouble putting his trousers on and Laraine was laughing at him stumbling around.

He found it even harder to brush his teeth, then a little later on he couldn't bring himself to eat his favourite bacon sandwich. And then... he became more confused, his speech was slurred, the left side of his face dropped, he was dribbling from one side of his mouth... it was at this point that he realised he was having a stroke.

At the age of 30, a strong and healthy, six foot plus, successful businessman, Owen had faced many challenges in his life but nothing quite like this.

"I was in the ambulance, when my arm fell off the stretcher. I couldn't move it and I knew that this was serious." He was being rushed to hospital and was close to facing permanent disability or even death.

One in three people die from a stroke, one third will suffer disability and one third will recover. Luckily for Owen, because Laraine had noticed the symptoms of the stroke quickly, and North Staffordshire hospital had a specialist stroke unit, he was able to make a full recovery.

"Looking back, I had obviously been under lots of pressure at work; in fact I can remember coming home the Friday before my stroke, red in the face and worrying about work. I had been self-employed and running my own businesses for 12 years and perhaps I just couldn't see the stress building up."

But Owen had a critical choice; he could either look at what had happened as a massive negative, or as a positive. Owen chose the positive. "In a strange way it allowed me to press pause – stop the bus if you like. It was an excuse to inspect my life from a distance and do something different. In life you rarely get that chance, that opportunity."

"I was perhaps still floating on the euphoria of simply not dying! I realised that in the past I had been very good at imposing huge amounts of pressure and worry on myself."

"I knew that I had to do something different with my life. I had to maintain a positive mind-set. Underestimate the power of a positive attitude at your peril; it really made a difference to me."

"In the early weeks after my stroke, I went through a very dark patch. Laraine, my family and friends, helped me loads. I was told by my specialist that a balanced lifestyle was important. Avoiding stress, eating healthy food, good exercise... I made the decision to radically change my life."

"I was determined to regain my positivity; I would not let my stroke steal my life away from me. I decided to give up my business... it was terribly hard but I knew it was the right thing to do. I had had a warning shot, a defining point in my life."

Owen felt that his stroke had given him a new purpose and direction, almost a calling as to "what he had been put on this earth to do". He began doing speeches about his experience for the Stroke Association, Stroke Research and other charities. Laraine even appeared live on the BBC Breakfast show to talk about stroke awareness, and how the speed of treatment can make a massive difference to the future quality of life of the person concerned.

Owen had always thought that one day he would love to get a job working outside in the open air.. His dream has come true. He is now a site manager, cutting grass and hedges, maintaining trees and generally getting his hands dirty.

"I love it! The fresh air, the sunshine, the fun and laughs we have together. In fact you could say I swapped the boardroom for a wheelbarrow. I get literally zero stress now. I start work at nine and leave at five."

"When I think about it, I realise that I spent too much of my life worrying about how I was perceived by others. I had to be seen to be successful – the right suit, the right car, do you know what I mean? But I don't give a s**t any more what people think of me, in the nicest possible way!"

"I have a brilliant life balance now. I enjoy the simple things, I'm not always chasing goals. I love my job, but work is no longer the 'big everything'. I've even started raising chickens, geese and ducks."

In fact, Laraine says that they both appreciate the simple life more. "We have been through so much together in such a short time. It has made us stronger."

Owen proposed to Larraine the week after he came out of hospital and they married on 17th December later that year. Their love and their strong emotional bond are clear for all to see.

"I wouldn't be the man I am today without Laraine, in fact to tell the truth, I wouldn't even be alive! Sometimes something bad has to happen to make you appreciate things more."

Owen has made a full recovery, perhaps with the strange exception of developing the unique ability to swear in public places! He once again has that sparkle in his eye and a new thirst for success, but this time he is determined it won't take over his life.

Thoughts from the flames!

- Don't be afraid to make massive changes in your life

- Learn to appreciate the simple things

- Live every day as if it's your last, life is too short to die with regrets

- Make time and take time with your loved ones

- Remember work isn't the "big everything!"

Chapter 10
Lisa's story

Lisa had been feeling strange for quite some time. For over six months she had been getting pins and needles down her left side; she thought it must be a trapped nerve or something.

Every time she bent over the sink or the bath she felt dizzy and really weird. Eventually she was so worried that she went to the doctor and he sent her for all sorts of tests. Finally the doctor told her the results.

"Lisa," he said slowly, "you have got MS."

"Thank God for that," said Lisa.

The doctor couldn't believe it and repeated what he said, "Do you understand, Lisa? You have MS – a chronic progressive disease of the central nervous system."

"I can handle that," she said, "I thought it was cancer or something!"

Some 10 years have passed since that conversation with her doctor and at the relatively young age of 43, Lisa has just been told she is slowly going blind and has been forced to give up work.

That news would be a huge shock to anybody, but as you will see Lisa is a very special lady indeed; somebody who has chosen to take a positive approach to her life and her own personal challenges.

"For a long time I didn't tell anybody about it. I didn't want to bother anybody about it or let them worry about it."

"But as it got worse I started to bump into things and my balance was affected; I finally had to tell my family. I try not to think about it. I just get on with my life. At the end of the day I could be run over by a bus tomorrow."

You see, like all of us, Lisa has choices in her life; she could easily have gone over to the dark side and sat back, given in and wallowed in depression. But Lisa chose a positive attitude to life and as she says, "At the end of the day it is a simple choice really; we can all choose the positive. We just have to be determined to live our lives to the full and appreciate every moment."

"I enjoy life. I get up every morning and think it's a new day, life's not a rehearsal. I can't understand why some people are so miserable and depressed all the time, yet they have everything; family, cars, money, a lovely house and their health. Why can't they just smile and appreciate what they have got? Have some fun – why be down when you've got your life to live."

I wonder if her positive attitude has been passed through her family?

Way back in the 60s Lisa's mum and dad had just been married at the age of 17 and 19. Her dad religiously did the football pools each week and gave her mum some money to get them for him on her way to work. Instead she bought some cigarettes. "She was dying for a fag," Lisa recalled, "and she thought it was a waste of money anyway and that they would never come in."

They did come in, all eight score draws and they would have won the jackpot! Sixty-two thousand pounds – an absolute fortune in those days.

When Lisa's mum got home she heard music and her dad was celebrating. After a while she built up the courage and told him the truth.

Although he was angry he just said, "What you ain't had you won't miss."

So perhaps that story has stuck in Lisa's mind. "Don't look for tomorrow... take it as it comes... you never know what is around the corner. Appreciate your family and the people around you."

What would have happened to their lives if her mum hadn't bought that packet of cigarettes? We will never know. But one thing is for sure... Lisa is determined to keep making the best of her life, helping people around her and appreciating every day.

Lady Lisa you are an inspiration!

Thoughts from the flames!

Choose a positive
attitude and live
everyday to the full.
After all, you never
know what is
around the corner!

Chapter 11
Mike's story

It was 3rd March 2009 when Mike locked the gates of the depot for the final time before the receivers were called in.

To say it was a shock to him was an understatement. He was made redundant along with 600 people. The impact on them, their families and the local community, was devastating.

Mike had worked as a Plant and Transport Manager for 30 years in a civil engineering business that at one time had been successfully turning over 100 million pounds a year.

"Things were bad and we could see it coming but it was still a massive shock," said Mike.

"The future was daunting, and frightening. I just didn't know where I would go or what I would do."

After a couple of months out of work Mike found another job with the company that took over the old transport business; only it meant he would be working away from home.

He had found new work but was now living over 150 miles away from his partner Eileen. At first things weren't too bad but Mike quickly became unhappy at living in hotels, and frustrated at the lack of support and help from his new employers.

"It was just a build-up of a number of little things really. Everything was completely different from what I was used to. The manager used to humiliate people if they did anything wrong. There was a different, almost vindictive culture, and I didn't know the area or the people. I began to hate every minute of it. It wasn't a nice place to work and one day, after an incident with a colleague where he kept blaming me over and over for something, I knew I had had enough!"

"That night I didn't sleep and just paced up and down in my hotel room. I couldn't think; I was numb with worry and feeling totally confused. My head had gone and I knew I was losing it. Finally, I just thought – I can't do this any more."

"In the morning I got on the first train possible and was home by 12:30pm that afternoon."

Mike knew he had left his job without another one to go to but he was tired, confused and suffering from a terrible bad back, possibly the result of stress and anxiety.

The doctor signed him off work and even made him complete a questionnaire to see if he was suicidal. He was suffering from severe depression; he didn't want to go out, see anybody or do anything. He just felt like his whole life and body was closing down.

"If it wasn't for Eileen I don't know what would have happened... I could have lost her and everything. I can't thank her enough for what she did."

But Eileen was a very determined lady. "I wasn't going to let us throw away everything that we had worked so hard for," she said. "I knew that Mike had lost his purpose and the routine in his life. He had been working at the same place for 30 years and his whole life pattern had changed. I knew I had to help him put some stability, discipline and structure back."

Eileen began to set him daily tasks and jobs. At first it was just a case of getting him out of bed, showered and dressed but soon he began to do more things around the house. As Mike started to feel a little bit better they even ordered a big wood cabin and he built it himself in their garden. Building the cabin became a passion for both of them and they loved to see it slowly being pieced together.

It had been an incredibly difficult year but Mike eventually got a job as a caretaker at a local infant and primary school.

"I love my new job and it's a very different environment from the madness and long hours of civil engineering. The kids, teachers and headmaster are all great. I like working with people the way they should be – nice and polite – people who appreciate and thank you for what you do."

"I wish I had done it 10 years ago! The money we used to have was nice but it's not everything in life. I am calmer and more patient now. At the end of the day I know that my dark time was just a little blip and that many people suffer from depression all their lives. But I owe everything to Eileen for pulling me around."

"We have more time for each other now: cooking, listening to music, enjoying the simple things. It's like when we first met 11 years ago; I have got the real Mike back," said Eileen. "Somebody said to me the other day... 'I can see you are happy because you have started to laugh again'."

Mike and Eileen have been on an incredibly difficult journey. But because of their love and the strength of their relationship they have come through it together. Mike is fit and healthy, has lost nearly 2 stone and looks years younger.

The strange thing is that while he was building his wood cabin he was also rebuilding his life, and regaining the passion and strength to continue along life's ever-changing path.

Mike's back and thanks to Eileen – he's smiling again!

Thoughts from the flames!

- Listen to and accept the help of those closest to you

- Enjoy the simple things together

- Never ever give up

- Remember that money isn't everything in life

The story behind the Fire Philosophy

Liam's story

When we began writing The Fire Philosophy we were determined to look a little deeper at some of the darker sides of life and how people cope with adversity.

Everybody at some time is faced with challenges and hardship but it is how we react to them that is important.

My mum brought me up as a single parent and was an incredible, motivational influence on me. She survived domestic violence at the hands of my dad who became addicted to prescribed drugs, chose a path to the dark, chaotic side of life, and eventually committed suicide.

I often think we are made and shaped by our family and the people we share our lives with. It is without doubt that but for the fierce determination and love of my mum I would never have made anything of my life.

Although my dad had a terrible side to his character he was also talented, charismatic and charming. He is a constant reminder to me that at any time, any one of us, can give in to life's pressures.

The people I have met in this book are an inspiration to me. Thanks James, Owen and Larraine, Lisa, and Mike and Eileen for your time. You have all shared amazing stories of courage, hope and love.

Everybody has a story to tell really, and most importantly everybody has a life to live.

Enjoy your life and roll with the good times and the bad...Why not? At the end of the day it makes sense to me!

Steve's story

While putting this book together with Liam it gave me a chance to reflect on my own life. Yes, like most people, there have been times in my life when things have been difficult... losing my job, my son contracting and recovering from meningitis, and a couple of family bereavements. But compared with the real life stories in this book I guess I've had things easy.

When you read the stories of James, Owen, Lisa and Mike, it makes you realise just how lucky you are and how you take the basic things in life for granted. It's often the case in life that you look at the things you want rather than what you already have. Your family, your home, your health and the basics like food and clothes, are some of the things most of us take for granted in our lives.

Sometimes it's only when a change in our life occurs that we realise just what we have. And if you don't already have what you want, then there is really only one person who can do something about it, and that's you.

**What people are saying about
'My fire's gone out!'...**

66 *Modern life can drain your energy and
confuse your mind. 'My fire's gone out!'
can guide you on a new positive direction.* 99

66 *'My fire's gone out!' out is an excellent
parable for our times, best book of the year
so far.* 99

66 *I've got to make a big decision and it's
helped me to think more logically and
productively about how I move forward.* 99

66 *I read it and immediately realised I could
embrace the change rather than be afraid
of it.* 99

66 *There is great value to be had in sharing this
book as a training tool to get some key
messages across to your people. Highly
recommended.* 99

" *The parable style of the book made me think about changes in life facing me, in a way the many "How to Cope with ... " books have never held my attention.* "

" **I would definitely recommend this book to anyone who is experiencing change in their lives or about to make changes.** "

" *It really makes you sit back and take stock of your own life, how you are coping with the day to day living of it and how you may be able to change the way you feel about what's happening just by adjusting your reactions to change.* "

" **If you get worn down by the pressures of work and your passion gets low, this is the book to relight your fire!** "

Reviews taken from Amazon.co.uk